Body Snatching

... of ...
Elizabeth ...
... Jan. 11, 18...

BODY SNATCHING

*The Robbing of Graves for the
Education of Physicians in
Early Nineteenth Century America*

by
Suzanne M. Shultz

McFarland & Company, Inc., Publishers
Jefferson, North Carolina, and London

*This book is dedicated to six people who have made a difference—
David A. Smith, M.D., Charles T. Young, O. Richard Forsythe,
Mrs. Cathy R. Deitz, Mrs. Martha Roddy—and
to the memory of Mrs. Eliza Armstrong.*

Frontispiece: The burial marker of Ruth Sprague, a young victim of body snatching, in Maple Grove Cemetery, Hoosick Falls, New York. Her tombstone preserves for all time the names of those who desecrated her grave and remains.

The present work is a reprint of the library bound edition of Body Snatching: The Robbing of Graves for the Education of Physicians in Early Nineteenth Century America, *first published in 1992 by McFarland.*

LIBRARY OF CONGRESS CATALOGUING-IN-PUBLICATION DATA

Shultz, Suzanne M.
    Body snatching: the robbing of graves for the education of physicians in early nineteenth century America / by Suzanne M. Shultz.
        p.   cm.
    Includes bibliographical references and index.

    ISBN 0-7864-2232-7 (softcover : 50# alkaline paper)

    1. Body snatching—United States—History. I. Title.
[DNLM: 1. Cadaver. 2. Dissection—history—United States.
3. Education, Medical—history—United States. WZ 320 S562b]
RA637.S58   2005
364.1'8–dc20
DNLM/DLC for Library of Congress   90-53522

British Library cataloguing data are available

Cover photograph ©2005 Photodisc

Manufactured in the United States of America

*McFarland & Company, Inc., Publishers
Box 611, Jefferson, North Carolina 28640
www.mcfarlandpub.com*

CONTENTS

Preface   vii
Introduction   ix

The Horrors of Dissection   1
Post Mortems and Anatomies in the Colonies   9
Dissection for Education   14
Resurrection of the Dead   26
American Professionals   59
Murder!   69
The Coming of the Anatomy Acts   78
The Decline of the Body Snatchers   90
Popular Literature   95
Appendix A: "History of the Anatomy Act of Pennsylvania,"
    by William Smith Forbes, M.D., 1867   111
Appendix B: Reports of Societies from the *Cincinnati*
    Lancet and Clinic, The Academy of Medicine
    on the Anatomy Act   117

Annotated Bibliography   119
Index   131

PREFACE

This book was not planned. It grew out of an idea for a paper on the history of post mortems in the United States and was to have been presented at Polyclinic Medical Center's Medical Education Day, an annual program where research papers are read. At first, the intrusion of the body snatchers was merely bothersome. Then, it became a fascination. The paper on post mortems never came to fruition but a paper titled "Body Snatchers" was presented and was well received. It originally encompassed only Pennsylvania laws and events. The final product is a bit wider in scope.

A great deal of material on body snatching is available, but it is neither easily accessible nor consistently indexed. It transects the lines of medical history, regional history, and general interest. Most of the recorded activity occurred in Great Britain and Scotland and literature is heavily weighted to those occurrences. For the most part, American literature appears in newspapers, medical journals, and pamphlets. Newspapers are not indexed; pamphlets are randomly cited; medical indexing is vague.

Histories are usually thought to be dry and boring. History is the faithful, impartial record of events, a recitation of unembellished facts. It assigns neither blame nor praise for the incidents that have gone on before. But for all that, it need not be stilted or dull. For history is also the record of activities of *people*. They lived, and had human characteristics just as our friends and colleagues. They laughed and cried, bled and died. This book is a compilation of certain activities of the last two centuries, a portrait of an undeniable part of medical history. It makes no moral judgments. From our vantage point in the 20th century, we can not fully know or understand the pressure for medical knowledge that drove young physicians to commit the acts detailed here. Any criticism would, therefore, be problematical.

vii

This, then, is an historical narrative or story. It is grounded in fact, but it is exciting, fascinating, tragic, appalling, and sometimes gruesome. Very little in this volume is "new" but the compilation of so many incidents in one monograph is unique. It is, I hope, readable, and perhaps even thrilling.

My intention in putting this monograph together has not been to produce a dissertation. It is meant to be, as a friend so succinctly described, a form of painless learning. Although when taken as a whole, the book traces the development of body snatching in a more or less chronological fashion, it is divided into short segments that can be read out of context and still retain a sense of story.

The documents quoted throughout this text retain their original spelling, punctuation, and capitalization. An annotated bibliography appears at the end of the book. Although it is intended to be as comprehensive as possible, this book is very probably incomplete. Many incidents such as those reported here have remained hidden for decades and will surface only by accident. Some have been concealed intentionally.

I am indebted to a number of friends and colleagues who have helped to make this book possible: Evelyn Andrews, law librarian; McNees, Wallace and Nurick, attorneys at law; Johanna Grimes, proprietor, Old Hickory Bookshop; Carolyn J. Hardnett, chief librarian, *Baltimore Sun*; Rosemary C. Barfield, *Michigan Quarterly Review*; Tom Horrocks, curator of the Historical Collection, College of Physicians of Philadelphia; Kathryn Ray, reference department, District of Columbia Public Library; Dorothy Provine, archivist, District of Columbia Archives; Samuel W. Berkheiser, M.D., retired director of laboratories, Polyclinic Medical Center; Jim Wood, photojournalist, Polyclinic Medical Center; and the reference librarians at the East Shore Branch of the Dauphin County Library System; The George T. Harrell Library, The Milton S. Hershey Medical Center, Pennsylvania State University; Cincinnati Historical Society Library in Eden Park, Cincinnati, Ohio; and the Public Library of Cincinnati and Hamilton County.

Finally, I need to thank my friends, who suffered through innumerable body snatcher stories over lunch, and my mother, who managed to cope with mountains of paper and countless evenings alone while I labored over research.

Sue Shultz
Fall 1991

INTRODUCTION

The purpose of this book is to present a vivid, lively, and readable portrait of the practice of grave robbing for the medical education of American medical students and physicians during the late 1700s and 1800s in the United States. Explanations of why the practice existed, how disinterment of corpses was accomplished, and who committed these acts are recounted. Whenever possible, one or more actual reported cases of body snatching are used to illustrate. Public and private efforts to prevent grave robbing are related. A chapter has been included on American professional grave robbers, a group of characters that have remained largely unknown in American history. This short passage on professional body snatchers might only scratch the surface of a much more widespread activity. Of particular importance is the rediscovery of George Christian, alias Dr. S.E. French, and his diary, both forgotten for more than a century. A brief look at European practices of dissection and body snatching are set forth, inasmuch as their experience predates, yet parallels, the American experience. Public attitudes and religious objections, as well as a sample of the popular literature of grave robbing, are also chronicled. A selection of the state laws together with the forces that motivated enactment are retold. The eventual decline of grave robbing and the reasons that it died out are speculated.

Although the collection is entitled *Body Snatching*, a number of other terms are used interchangeably throughout this volume. *Resurrectioning* or *resurrectionists*, *grave robbers*, *fishermen*, *snatches*, *grabs*, and *sack-em-up-men* also refer to the practice of illegal disinterment of human remains and the persons who perform the work. Body snatching is the most descriptive in that would-be thieves took only bodies (sometimes referred to as "things" or "stiffs") for their purposes, leaving behind all of the personal effects that were buried with the deceased. Grave robbing for the motive of obtaining jewelry or other valuables buried with the deceased is beyond the scope of this book and has not been dealt with herein. Stealing only the body from the grave was not considered a felony since it has been judged that a dead body can have no owner. Therefore, the grave clothes were usually returned to the coffin to avoid any criminal wrongdoing. Resurrection is a colorful description of a cemetery raid to raise a body from the dead to be used for the study of anatomy. Lonsdale (p. 55) suggests that the term "resurrectionists" came about because it was commonly believed that the burial ground was sacred and that the removal of a body from "God's Acre" was interference with the plan of Providence and the great Resurrection. Thus resurrectionists and body snatchers became synonymous terms.

A term common to the turn of the century was *burking,* after William Burke, an Irish criminal. To burke is "to suffocate or strangle in order to obtain a body to be sold for dissection." The story of the murders of William Burke and William Hare appears in a later chapter. A short version of Burke's exploits can be found in Bettman, *Pictorial History of Medicine.* A more detailed account is included in Ball, *The Sack-'Em-Up Men* and Barzun, *Burke and Hare: The Resurrection Men, A Collection of Contemporary Documents Including Broadsides, Occasional Verses, Illustrations, Polemics, and a Complete Transcript of the Testimony at the Trial.* In addition to these and other historical accounts of Burke and Hare, there are numerous fictionalized versions of their reprehensible actions. None are more horrifying than the truth. Although considerable publicity has surrounded the three English burking scandals, almost no attention has been drawn to the American murders for the supply of bodies to medical schools. The United States can claim, most disgracefully, two such cases which resulted in the surrender of a total of four cadavers to medical schools. In both instances, the perpetrators profited monetarily in the short term but paid with their own lives for their crimes.

THE HORRORS OF DISSECTION

The Art Anatomists of the 15th Century

The art anatomists were among the first to practice dissections. They were primarily interested in anatomy for form and function to assist their creative skills. The advantage that they had over their medical counterparts was that they were not influenced by the foibles and biases in thinking of those that had passed before. Their work is an exact replica of what they saw. They watched medical dissections when possible but many conducted dissections themselves either publicly or secretly.

Antonio Pollaiuolo (ca. 1431–1498) is usually credited with being the first painter to have dissected human corpses. In addition to painting, he was a sculptor, silversmith, tapestry designer, and teacher. Probably his most famous work is a sculpture entitled *Hercules and Antaeus*, the detail of which is dynamic. The engraving (his only one) that clearly gives insight into his dissecting activities is *The Battle of the Ten Nudes*. The figures almost appear to have been skinned; the underlying musculature is an excellent representation of true anatomic configuration. Luca Signorelli (1442–1524) was a student of Pollaiuolo and was also an art anatomist. It is said that he visited burial grounds to collect body parts. Michelangelo admired him.

Two other artists who were also anatomists and are far better known than Pollaiuolo are Michelangelo Buonarroti and Leonardo da Vinci. Michelangelo (1475–1564) has no peer where representations of the human figure are concerned. His paintings in the Sistine Chapel are the perfected

1

works of a lifelong study of the human form assisted by anatomical dissections. He studied anatomy at Florence and Rome and was a great friend of Realdo Colombo (1516–1559), an anatomist who succeeded Andreas Vesalius. Leonardo (1452–1519) is known primarily for his paintings although he was also an architect and sculptor. His anatomical work, which appeared in his notebooks and consisted of some 120 folios, was not published until the 1800s. It was disorganized, included notes and other memoranda, and was sometimes contradictory. John Hunter felt that Leonardo was the best anatomist in the world at his time and that his sketches and observations, even though obsolete, were excellent. *Leonardo da Vinci, the Anatomist* by J. Playfair McMurrich contains many plates from the notebooks and includes commentary on the drawings. The book addresses possible sources of Leonardo's anatomical knowledge as well as a systematic review of his work. The illustrations are beautiful.

An alliance between art and medicine was forged early and the tradition has continued to the present day. Artists and anatomists worked together to produce some of the finest medical works available. Andreas Vesalius was said to have used the artist Calcar, a disciple of Titian, to produce the plates for his magnum opus, *Fabrica*. Artists also studied with anatomists. Michelangelo was the student of Realdo Colombo, who succeeded Vesalius at the University at Padua.

If early anatomical study could be arbitrarily grouped, it would probably best fall into three areas: gross anatomy, or what is visible to the naked eye; pathological anatomy, or the correlation of clinical (disease state) observations with anatomical evidence; and surgical anatomy, the study of the repair by surgery of altered anatomic conditions caused by disease. These general classifications also translate into three eras. The first (gross anatomy) is represented by Andreas Vesalius and the University of Padua. The second (pathological anatomy) is typified by the University of Leyden. The last (surgical anatomy) began with Alexander Monro, Primus at the University of Edinburgh.

Andreas Vesalius and the University at Padua

Although Padua produced many fine physician-anatomists, the most famous was Andreas Vesalius. Born in Brussels in 1514, Vesalius took his degree from Padua and, upon completion of his degree, immediately assumed a professorship in surgery there. He was a mere 23 years of age. One of the duties of this position was to conduct public dissections from time to time, but Vesalius did not stop there. He conducted numerous studies on animals and humans, both in public and in private, on bodies obtained either legally or illicitly. In 1538, his first anatomical work was published, a series of six plates intended to aid his students in their studies. His monumental achievement was published just five years later in 1543 and was entitled *De Humani Corporis Fabrica*. Vesalius was then 28. *Fabrica* consisted of 663 pages. In it, Vesalius addressed human anatomical discrepancies which he had found in Galen's works. Through his own research, he had discovered that much of Galen's writing was based on comparative anatomy, animal rather than human, and that it was written entirely without knowledge of dissected human remains. Vesalius's work verifies that 16th century anatomists were investigating and demonstrating on human bodies. Vesalius is the father of modern anatomy and very probably the greatest figure in Renaissance medicine. He was followed at Padua by Gabriel Fallopius, a protégé, whose contributions to the study of anatomy have immortalized his name. Fallopius further refined *Fabrica* in 1561 with his own *Observationes Anatomicae*. Also from Padua is Guilio Casseri (1552–1616), an anatomist and lecturer, who wrote *Tabulae Anatomicae* in 1627. He is noted for his descriptions of the organs of speech and hearing. Adrian Spigelius (1567–1625), a teacher of anatomy at Padua from 1618–1624, was an excellent surgeon as well.

The University at Leyden

From the Northern Italian schools, the center of anatomical learning next passed north to the University at Leyden (or Leiden). The Paduans' inquiry into anatomy seems to have lost the interest of the scientific community. The clinical study of both natural and disease states in correlation with anatomic findings became the next focus of medical attention. The Dutch were distinguished for their anatomists, and a number of paintings by well-known artists depict dissections. Two by Rembrandt are *The Lesson in Anatomy of Dr. Johan Deyman* and *The Lesson in Anatomy of Dr. Tulp*. The Deyman painting shows two people engaged in a dissection. Although it is apparent that the body is open, it is difficult to discern any details. The position of the figures and the anatomical detail of the painting resemble another earlier painting titled *The Death of Christ* by Andrea Mantegna (1431–1506) except that the body of Christ is not open. Tulp, on the other hand, depicts seven onlookers and one demonstrator surrounding a cadaver in the beginning stages of dissection. Another less famous painting is that of Juriaen Pool entitled *Boekelman, President of the Society of Surgeons showing a colleague, Six, a Heart with Injected Arteries*. The heart is that of a human and the arteries projecting from it are quite clear.

In 1597 Pieter Paaw, professor of anatomy and botany, founded the first Dutch anatomical theater at Leyden. A fine engraving of the theater was done by Andreas Stog in 1589. However, it was probably Anton van

Leeuwenhoek's (1632–1723) discovery of the microscope that caused the transfer of anatomical study to Leyden. Many of the professors and anatomists of Leyden have carved their place in medical history. Philip Verheyen (1647–1710) published a treatise on anatomy in 1693 which contained microscopic studies. Hermann Boerhaave (1668–1738) was an outstanding clinician and teacher. Boerhaave recognized the importance of matching clinical symptoms with pathological changes seen at autopsy. His post mortem examinations led to the original description of a ruptured esophagus. Boerhaave's syndrome is the rupture of the esophagus with leakage of the gastric contents into the mediastinum. Bernhard Siegfried Albinus (1697–1770) was an anatomist and instructor in dissection who, with Boerhaave, reissued Vesalius's works. Albinus also published a number of his own anatomical studies, which are exact and detailed representations. His greatest production was an eight-volume to me entitled *Academicarum Annotationium* which included anatomy, psychology, pathology, physiology, zoography and phytography. This work was published over a period of years from 1754 through 1768. Johann Jacob Wepfer (1620–1695) discovered the association between brain hemorrhage and stroke. Regnier de Graaf (1641–1673) was an anatomist known for his work on digestion, but his most lasting discovery was the ovarian follicle, which bears his name. He published two works of note: *De Virorum Organis Generationi Inservientibus* in 1668, and *De Mulierum Organis Generationi Inservientibus Tractatus Novus*, in 1672. De Graaf was interested in van Leeuwenhoek's microscope but was never able to use the instrument in his own studies. He died of the plague in the summer of 1673 at the age of 32.

Alexander Monro, Primus, and the University of Edinburgh

From Leyden, the center of anatomic teaching passed to the University at Edinburgh in the person of Alexander Monro Primus in 1720. Monro was a surgical apprentice to his father John Monro and later completed his medical education in London, Paris, and Leyden. His personal papers record his attendance at classes on clinical surgery and anatomy, performing at least eight dissections during his matriculation (Lawrence p. 195–196). Upon returning home in 1719 to Edinburgh, he began to teach a course in anatomy (at the age of 22), a vocation to which he proved to be well suited. Monro wrote his course outline and description of anatomical dissection with meticulous care. The course began with a history of anatomy, some physiology, and comparative anatomy. His writings contain detailed instructions for the preservation and preparation of cadavers, as well as the technique of and the composition of the fluid used for injection of the corpse. Since a cadaver had to last for a long time, he provided instructions on prevention or reduction of wasting away of the tissue. With so lengthy a course and only a limited supply of bodies, prevention of decay had to be of serious concern. He listed the anatomist's armamentarium including knives, scissors, pipes, tubes, saws, drills, wires, injecting apparatus and microscope (Lawrence p. 199).

His lecture began with the study of bones, and progressed to the study of organic structure and relationship. He followed a specific plan of anatomical examination with each cadaver, progressing in an orderly fashion through all of the organ systems. With the first cadaver, he dissected muscles, tendons, and ligaments. The second cadaver was used to lecture on the nervous and circulatory systems since these were destroyed by dissection of the muscles in the first.

Monro's entire course, from October to April, was executed with only two cadavers. He was an extremely popular teacher almost from his first undertaking and the attendance at his lectures numbered from 60 to 200 students (Lawrence p. 195). It is quite obvious from the size of the classes and the paucity of bodies that anatomy was absorbed by demonstration. It was this method of teaching that eventually caused students to look elsewhere for their anatomical training. William Hunter's school espoused participatory education, a cadaver for every student. And with the change in philosophy began the quest for more human bodies.

The United States

The medical profession in the United States achieved its renowned stature only fairly recently. Throughout the colonial period and until well after the Civil War, well-educated physicians were those who traveled to Europe to attain excellence in the art and science of medicine. Early contributors to the profession were usually graduates of Edinburgh and, to a lesser extent, the German and French schools. John Morgan, William Shippen, Jr., Benjamin Waterhouse, and Samuel Bard, to name a few, were educated in Edinburgh. Some insight into the perceived state of American cultural and scientific development is seen in the commentary of Sydney Smith written for the *Edinburgh Review* in 1820. Following are some of Mr. Smith's observations:

> The Americans are a brave, industrious, and acute people, but they have hitherto made no approaches to the heroic, either in their morality or their character. During the thirty or forty years of their independence, they have done absolutely nothing for the sciences, for the arts, for literature, or even for the statesmanlike studies of politics and political economy ... *In the four corners of the globe, who reads an American book? or*

goes to an American play? or looks upon an American picture or statue?
What does the world yet owe to American physicians or surgeons? What
new substances have their chemists discovered, or what old ones have
they analyzed? What new constellations have been discovered by the
telescopes of Americans? What have they done in mathematics? Who
drinks out of American glasses, or eats out of American plates, or wears
American coats or gowns, or sleeps in American blankets?

Although young physicians returned from studies abroad with the en-
thusiasm and determination to establish educational excellence equal to or
exceeding those they attended, the American experience was different.
Regretfully, there was some merit to Sydney Smith's scathing remark. A
few splendid scientific accomplishments from the pre–1850 period exist but
they are the exception rather than the rule for American medicine. Medical
schools grew in wildcat proportions while the standard of education remained generally poor or perhaps even declined. Medicine floundered
amidst the Jacksonian democratic influence of sectarians, herbalists, patent
medicine peddlers, eclectics and quacks until the American Medical
Association assumed leadership in 1847. Only then did American medicine
accede to the esteem in which it is viewed today.

The glory of the new American medical tradition was captured on can-
vas by Philadelphian Thomas Eakins (1844–1916). As a young man, Eakins
studied anatomy under William Pancoast, M.D., at Jefferson Medical College in 1864–1865. He then studied art and painting abroad, first in France
from 1866–1869, then in Spain. He returned to Philadelphia in 1870 and
became acquainted with Dr. William W. Keen, who taught anatomy at the
Pennsylvania Academy of Fine Arts. By 1879, Eakins himself was teaching
the anatomical dissection course to students. He commented, "To draw the
human figure it is necessary to know as much as possible about it, about
its structure and its movements, its bones and muscles, how they are made,
and how they act . . . we turn out no physicians and surgeons . . . but we
are considerably concerned about learning how to paint" (Brieger). A self-
portrait of Eakins appears in both of his well-known paintings, *The Portrait
of Professor Gross (The Gross Clinic)* (1875) and *The Agnew Clinic* (1889).
Samuel David Gross, M.D., and David Hayes Agnew, M.D., were giants
of the surgery profession of their day. The paintings, at Jefferson Medical
College and University of Pennsylvania respectively, are accurate in detail
and realistic in portrayal. There are strong contrasts in lighting between the
surgical theater and the gallery in both pictures, but the most noticeable
difference in the two pictures is the lack of surgical gowns in the earlier
Gross Clinic. In the intervening 14 years between the paintings, the surgical
profession had changed some of its attitudes concerning sepsis and technique and these are reflected in the change in surgical garb.

Medical leadership passed from Edinburgh to a young but maturing

United States, and with it the responsibility for excellence in medical education. Anatomical knowledge was viewed here, as abroad, as the cornerstone of a sound medical education. The shortage of cadavers was no less acute a problem than it had been in other antecedent medical centers of learning. American management of the situation was just as inexpedient as that of our European predecessors.

Religious Objections

Although religious objections are often cited as the primary reason for denying the use of human cadavers for the study of anatomy by dissection/autopsy, there are no specific Catholic or Protestant prohibitions against the practice. Evidence of the broad-minded views of the Catholic church on autopsy is apparent in the work of the early Italian anatomists and writers. Indeed, a post mortem was performed on Pope Alexander V in 1410. The Vatican drew the line during the Crusades when the bodies of those who died were dismembered, boiled, macerated, and the bones sent home. Even though the motivation for the practice was to assure a proper burial, it was judged barbaric and therefore prohibited by papal bull.

Orthodox Judaism forbids autopsy, but there are references to dissections or other anatomical descriptions in Hebrew literature. Jewish physicians of the 16th and 17th centuries conducted autopsies. By the 1700s, rabbinical interpretation was that although autopsy was forbidden by Jewish law, if it could be shown that performance of dissection could save a life, exception might be made. The interpretation was not to permit autopsy for the good of all mankind or for future advancement of medical knowledge, but for the critically ill patient who may benefit directly from anatomical examination of the deceased person's remains. Furthermore, a full autopsy is not countenanced when a limited one, i.e., examination of the organs in situ, may serve to answer specific questions. The basis for Biblical prohibition is found in Deuteronomy 21:22–23: "And if a man has committed a crime punishable by death and he is put to death, and you hang him on a tree, his body shall not remain all night upon the tree, but you shall bury him the same day, for a hanged man is accursed by God; you shall not defile your land which the Lord your God gives you for an inheritance."

Two thoughts are worthy of note. Most grave robbing occurred in Protestant countries although it does not appear that religious inclination was a consequential factor. Because of the Jewish burial practice of same-day interment of the dead, these cadavers would have been especially attractive to anatomists and resurrectionists owing to their freshness. Before embalming was practiced widely, specimens deteriorated rapidly, severely limiting their period of usefulness.

Criminality

The legal acquisition of cadavers for dissection was constrained by public attitude. The history of anatomy related to criminality dates back to Scotland where dissections merely completed the work begun by the gallows. The horror of additional revenge beyond death was laid at the door of the surgeons and anatomists who carried out the "sentence." Thus, dissection was viewed with revulsion by the community at large. Autopsy was considered a religious sacrilege, a great indignity imposed upon social outcasts, and an extra punishment beyond death.

Because dissection was permitted on the bodies of criminals, unclaimed bodies, and in Massachusetts (1784), on the victims of duels and their murderers, the practice became associated with criminality in the United States as well. The text of the Massachusetts law concerning dissection is as follows:

> When it shall appear by coroner's inquest that any person hath been killed in fighting a duel, the coroner of the county where the fact was committed shall be directed and empowered to take effectual care that the body of such person so killed be immediately secured and buried without a coffin, with a stake drove through the body, at or near the usual place of execution, or shall deliver the body to any surgeon or surgeons, to be dissected and anatomized, that shall request the same and engage to apply the body to that use. ... That any person who shall slay or kill another in a duel, and shall, upon conviction thereof on an indictment for murder, receive sentence of death, part of the judgment of the court shall be that the body be delivered to any surgeon or surgeons, to be dissected and anatomized, that shall appear in a reasonable time after execution to take the body, and engage to apply it to that purpose.

This 1784 act was not intended to "legalize" the study of anatomy nor the practice of human dissection, but rather to make dueling as unattractive as possible. Massachusetts did not officially sanction nor recognize the need for dissection and study of anatomy until 1831. In 1788 Virginia refused to permit the dissection of executed murderers (Hartwell p. 218). In 1789, New York provided bodies for dissection with a law that allowed the court "at their discretion [to] add to the judgment that the body of such offender [those convicted of a crime and sentenced to death] shall be delivered to the surgeons for dissection." New Jersey followed with a similar law in 1796 (Hartwell p. 218). The following year the United States Congress allowed federal judges the same power in cases of murder (Packard p. 298–301). It is not surprising that legislatures were indifferent or reluctant to deal with the problem of shortage of cadavers for medical teaching.

*For those who have dissected or
inspected many, have at least learn'd to
doubt when the others, who are ignorant
of anatomy, and do not take the trouble to
attend it, are in no doubt at all.*
                    — Giovanni Battista Morgagni
                                    (1682–1771)

POST MORTEMS AND ANATOMIES IN THE COLONIES

Many examples of early legal post mortems fill the historical medical literature. Marmaduke Percy was arraigned in 1639 in Massachusetts for the death of an apprentice who was dissected after his death. The boy probably died of skull fracture. John Dandy of Maryland shot and killed an Indian boy named Edward in 1643 (Steiner p. 201-2). The report to the jury included details of a post mortem examination as follows: "We find this Indian (named Edward) came to his death by a bullett shot by John Dandy which bullett entered the epigastrum near the navel on the right side, obliquely descending and piercing the gutts, glancing on the last vertebra of the back, and was lodged in the side of Ano. Signed George Binx" (Spiro p. 103). Binx was the jury foreman and had some medical experience himself. In 1662, Dr. Bryan Rossiter examined 8-year-old Elizabeth Kelley's body for evidence of death by witchcraft. The child died on March 26, 1662, and the post mortem was conducted on March 31, 1662. Rossiter apparently felt that the child had succumbed to supernatural causes (Hoadley p. 211-216). He reported, "The whole body, the musculous parts, nerves and joints were all pliable, without any stiffness or contraction, the gullett only excepted. Experience of dead bodies render such symptoms unusual" (Steiner; Spiro p. 105). Dr. Rossiter's experience with death and the passing of rigor with time must have been very limited or entirely lacking. Modern day speculation is that the changes observed by Rossiter were normal anatomical decay and putrefaction.

A post mortem examination was conducted by John Stansley and John Peerce on Benjamin Price on August 8, 1670, in Maryland. Mr. Price was allegedly killed by Indians. The deaths of John Bridge of Roxbury, Massachusetts, deceased August 20, 1674, and Jacob Goodale, Salem, June 1, 1676, were investigated by autopsy (Matthews p. 276). In 1675, there is a reference to the death of a man in the house of Giles Corey of Massachusetts who was bruised to death and had "clodders of blood about the heart" (Hartwell p. 212). A dissection was performed on an executed Indian in the presence of Judge Sewell on September 22, 1676. On May 2, 1678, a post mortem was done on the body of Edward Bodye in Salem, Massachusetts (Matthews p. 276).

Cotton Mather described two deaths in his own family where post mortems occurred but neither appears to have been demanded by law (Krumbhaar p. 809). On that of his sister, Katherine, he noted, "When she was opened, it was found, that the right lobe of her lungs was utterly wasted and not anything but about three quarters of a pint of quittor, in the room thereof. She was not a year old; and had lain sick for four or five months" (Matthews p. 277). In *Magnalia Christi Americana* Book III (p. 437), Mather notes of Mr. Samuel Stone, Doctor Irrefragabilis, that "if it were *metaphorically* true (what they *proverbially* said) of Beza, that 'he had no gall,' the physicians that opened him after his death found it literally true in this worthy man."

The celebrated case of Governor Slaughter of New York is usually cited as the first legal post mortem, which it is not. The governor died on July 23, 1691, under mysterious circumstances that some attributed to poisoning. A post was ordered on the day of his death. An excerpt from a letter dated August 6 reveals the cause for the order. "We must acquaint you that on the 23 Instant his Excellency Sloughter our governor departed this life in a very sudden manner, whose body we caused to be opened by the Physicians and Surgeons on the place; a copy of whose report to us upon their oaths we have herewith sent you, to which you will see their opinions concerning the cause of his death" (Matthews p. 277). Dr. Johannes Kerfbyle examined the body. Kerfbyle's description was that Slaughter "died of a defect in his blood and lungs occasioned by some glutinous tough humor in the blood, which stopped the passage thereof and occasioned its settling in the lungs" (Walsh: *History of Medicine in New York* p. 37). It may be that the honorable governor passed away from an ailment commonly known as pulmonary embolism.

On January 22, 1705, a post mortem was conducted on Elizabeth Whetlie to determine whether she was pregnant at the time of her death. She was (Matthews p. 277). Cotton Mather mentions another post in July 1716 on the body of his neighbor named Call. This man apparently died because "his bladder was grown entirely schirrous" (Matthews p. 278).

Samuel Clossy, who held the chair in anatomy at King's College in New York, later Columbia, wrote *Observations on Some of the Diseases*

of the Human Body , Chiefly Taken from the Dissections of Morbid Bodies
in 1763. Under the auspices of a mentor Dr. William Stephens, the "Observations" were the result of Dr. Clossy's research in anatomy on patients dying at Steevens' Hospital in Dublin. At a time when it was extremely difficult to obtain bodies for medical study, Dr. Stephens offered Dr. Clossy the opportunity to perform post mortems on the patients who died in the hospital. The book was published just before Clossy emigrated to the United States. The contents are based on post mortem examinations conducted from 1752 to 1756. In the preface of his book, Dr. Clossy wrote, "[K]nowledge of the affectations of the Human System is acquired by seeing symptoms and dissecting bodies, and both are improved by reason and reflection."

Having taken up residence in New York, Dr. Clossy submitted an advertisement to the newspaper of his intent to begin lectures in anatomy. The announcement of his course appeared in the *New York Mercury*.

King's College, October 26. 1767
On Monday November the Second, at Four O'clock in the Evening; the First Part of Dr. Clossy's Anatomical Lectures, will begin with the Usefulness of Anatomy; and will proceed to the Description of the Dry Bones, and likewise the Fresh Bones, with their Cartilages, Ligaments, and Membranes; Internal Structures, Uses, Motions, and Affections; and will be continued on every Friday and Monday ensuing.
After the First Part, the System of Muscles will be shewn in the Adult Subject.
Part the Third, will exhibit the Arteries, Veins, and Trunks of the Nerves, in a Subject, prepared with Injections: and the whole will be concluded with, The Fourth Part, containing the Encephalon, with the Vicera of the two inferior Cavities, together with their Uses, Motions, and Diseases, in an Adult Subject.
Attendance at each Course to the Students of Physick, Five Pounds; and free after Two Courses.
For seeing Dissections and Preparations, Ten Pounds, and free after Two Courses.
To Gentlemen who will chuse to attend for the Improvement of their Minds, Three Pounds Four Shillings...

In a letter dated November 1763, Clossy wrote to his great friend and teacher, Dr. George Cleghorn of Dublin, that he had begun Lectures in Anatomy in New York. Following are some excerpts from that letter:

...I procured first a Female who died of inflammation of the Bowels, (a disorder very common in this country,) and began (because I had no dry bones to begin regularly) with the muscles of the Lower belly and in succession went through the Contents of this Cavity; the Contents then of the Chest; and ended my first part with the Encephalon and its Membranes; explaining every evening the Structure as fibrous, vascular and nervous, and every succeeding, their uses motions and diseases.

Part the Second, began with a Black female, on which I went quite through the Muscles except those of the Uvula which I could not find partly from want of due experience and partly from the foetor of the Subject.

Part the third I could not compleat for want of a young subject for by this time myself and myrmydoms were so known in the place that we could not venture to meddle with a white subject, and a black or Mulatto I could not procure, so that I ended in forty-four nights, speaking as freely as if I had been a Lecturer for years.

The first subject was white, and about twenty; and as I said died of an Inflammation in the Stomach and Intestines; the Stomach was almost black with blood extravasated into the interstices of its fibres; the Small intestines quite black, putrid, and dry —

The second Subject a female black, had a very large Polypus in the right ventricle running into the Pulmonary Artery keeping open the Valves, there was another also in the left auricle and Ventricle, they were as much flesh as the heart itself, and about the thickness of my middle finger; the whole System of veins were exceedingly enlarged and turgid, the whole System of Muscles red as Scarlet, the consequence of these obstructions in the Heart — but one thing singular was the beautifull carving on the Neck breast and bely which 'tis impossible to describe Verbally, Hieroglyphics possible of the kingdom of Angola —

Since then, I dissected a Male Black, for the Sake of the Skeleton, he belonged to a friend of mine and died of gripes and a Jaundice, in the lower belly I found the small Intestines pale Yellow, Carneous, thick as the Colon, the diameter of my little finger, and filled with nought but yellow bile... [Smith p. 219–220; Stookey p. 166].

Thomas Cadwalader's manuscript entitled "An essay on the West-India Dry-Gripes; with the Method of Preventing and Curing that Cruel Distemper to which is added, An Extraordinary Case in Physic" is an excellent presentation on lead poisoning acquired by drinking rum distilled through lead pipes. The "extraordinary case" is a study of osteomalacia in a diabetic patient. Both of these reports were based on notes from post mortem examinations. The original report on osteomalacia is contained in Major's Classic Descriptions of Disease. Cadwalader's paper was printed and sold by Benjamin Franklin (1745) and is one of the earliest medical monographs in this country.

Dr. Thomas Cadwalader studied medicine in England and France. He acquired his anatomical expertise from Cheselden, and upon returning to the colonies, performed dissections for the elder Dr. Shippen and others who had not had the opportunity to study abroad. It is quite probable that Cadwalader was the first to have formally taught anatomy in Pennsylvania.

Other colonies followed Massachusetts, New York, and Pennsylvania. The first autopsies performed at the request of jury foremen in the state of Georgia were recorded in 1773. Dr. Andrew Johnston of Augusta was requested to examine the body of William Miller who had been shot to death. Dr. George Fraser performed a post mortem on Joseph Cox, who had been murdered. The first published autopsy record from Georgia appeared in 1805 and was penned by Dr. Joshua E. White of Savannah. He was assisted by Dr. John Grimes in the examination of the body of an 8-year-old child who was thought to have succumbed to internal hydrocephalus. Their study revealed degeneration of the "middle lobes" (of the brain?) and chronic apoplexy. In 1818, Dr. Alexander Ramsay presented a paper at the annual medical society meeting in which he described an autopsy of an infant with a diaphragmatic hernia (Krafka).

Public Anatomies

Credit for the first public anatomy in the United States is commonly assigned to Drs. John Bard and Peter Middleton. In 1750 in New York City, they performed a post mortem on Hermanus Carroll, an executed criminal. "[T]he blood vessels [were] injected for the instruction of the youth then engaged in the study of medicine; this was the first essay made in the United States for the purpose of imparting medical knowledge by the dissection of the human body, of which we have any record" (*American Medical and Philosophical Register* 2:228, 1812).

In fact, Carroll's post mortem was not the first recorded public anatomy. One occurred on or about March 22, 1733, on the body of Julian, an Indian. Julian murdered a man named John Rogers on September 12, 1732, by stabbing him to death. He was tried and executed for his crime. Details of the post mortem were reported by the Boston news. "The body of Julian the Indian man, who was executed here last week, having been granted several young students in physick, surgery, and etc. at their request; the same has for several days past been dissecting in their presence, in a most accurate manner; and it is hoped their critical inspection, will prove of singular advantage. The bones are preserved, in order to be framed into a skeleton" (Matthews p. 279).

Three other cases, one in 1734 and two in 1736, cited by Matthews appear to have been "public" anatomies and predate the Carroll anatomy by 14 years. Of these five, including Carroll, three were performed on the bodies of executed criminals.

DISSECTION FOR EDUCATION

The acquisition of bodies for medical teaching purposes was a decided impediment to 18th and 19th century physicians of England and the United States. The number of legally available corpses was woefully inadequate for the study of anatomy and the development of professional skills. The only legitimate sources of bodies were those of executed criminals and those bequeathed to medical schools for study. Simple comparison of the number of students and the number of legitimate bodies, coupled with the requirements for a medical degree, reveals the radical imbalance of available anatomic teaching material.

For a young United States, the problem began early. Pennsylvania claims the first medical school in the United States, the Medical Department of the University of Pennsylvania, established in 1765 through the efforts of William Shippen, Jr., and John Morgan. By the mid 1870s, there had been eleven schools chartered in the state; two combined to form a third, and one, the Independent Medical School of Pennsylvania, never opened for classes. Six of these medical schools provided regular curricula and by 1876, had graduated a total of 16,819 students (Billings in Clarke, p. 358). Since practical anatomy was usually a requirement for a medical degree or, if not required, the most popular of the elective subjects, over the 108 year period from 1768 to 1876, at the lowest estimate a probable 4,200 to 8,000 dissections took place. As many as 16,800 dissections may have occurred if a one-to-one, cadaver/student ratio is postulated. These numbers include only graduates and exclude students who enrolled but never achieved degrees. All of the schools except one were located in Philadelphia, as the search for bodies to dissect would have been largely confined to the city and surrounding suburban areas.

14

Waite (p. 276) estimates that during the 20-year period from 1820 to 1840, more than 1,600 medical students attended medical school in Vermont. Since all students were required to perform a dissection either as a group at a medical school or singly with a preceptor, at least 400 cadavers would have been necessary to meet the needs. During that time only one or two bodies per year were made available legally, a total of perhaps 40 at most. Some 360 of them must then have been obtained illegally.

Blake (p. 433) notes that Massachusetts executed only 26 persons from 1800 to 1830; the federal court for Massachusetts only 14 from 1789 to 1830. Again, 40 cadavers provided by law were scarcely enough to supply a single medical school in the state for one year.

Sozinsky estimated that the number of bodies required for anatomical teaching in the United States was about 5,000. In 1878, there were about 10,000 students in medical schools, about half of whom were graduated in the spring. Each young physician would have required at least one subject for dissection during his training. "Of these five thousand subjects, at least a majority are illegally obtained, many of them by actual purchase. A body will sell for five dollars anywhere, and in Ohio and other states thirty dollars is the usual price. Where it is easy to procure the necessary supply of subjects they are cheap; and where it is difficult, they are dear. Where bodies sell at a high price, graverobbing, and even burking, may be expected" (Sozinsky p. 216).

Lonsdale, in *A Sketch of the Life and Writings of Robert Knox*, commented that the acquisition of bodies was a major obstacle to the teaching of anatomy in Great Britain. He asserted that human bodies were essential to the practice of pathology and surgery. It was the English custom to provide bodies of executed criminals, and unclaimed dead of prisons and poorhouses for anatomical study. "Our legitimate source hardly amounts to units in the scale of wants, and is therefore totally inadequate; our professional status does not receive any recognition at the hands of the Legislature; and, in self-defense of interests, affecting the general weal more than ourselves, we are forced to associate with the most abandoned of characters — the Resurrectionists" (p. 57).

Medical training in the colonies and throughout the early history of the republic was acquired by the apprenticeship method. Before the establishment of medical schools, an aspiring young physician could only obtain a practical education through several years of service to a preceptor. In this setting, the student accompanied the physician on rounds, assisted in the care and treatment of patients, learned the art of communication through observance of the doctor-patient relationship, and observed the natural course of diseases. Most of the reading material at his disposal was out of date. Occasionally, the apprentice and preceptor would dissect an animal or a cadaver when the opportunity presented itself.

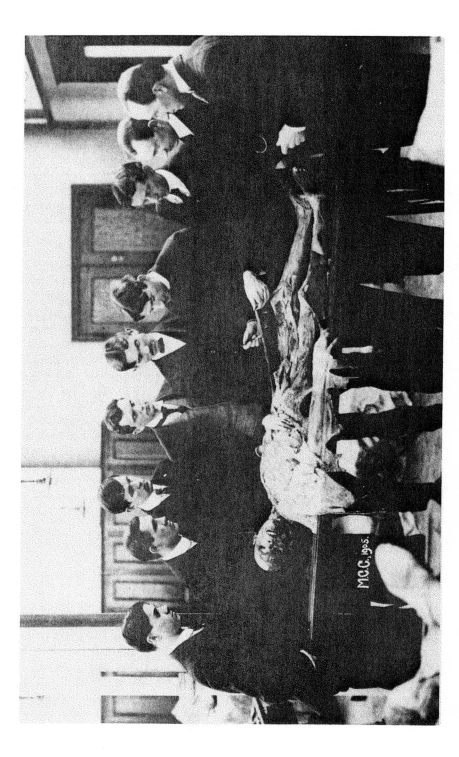

The medical education curriculum of the Royal College of Surgeons of England required five years of study. Apprenticeship was considered to be very important and students were encouraged to spend as much of the five years as they liked in this pursuit. In addition, students were required to attend two courses of lectures and demonstrations in anatomy at London, Dublin, Edinburgh, or Glasgow and to take two courses in practical dissection at an anatomical school. A year of clinical experience in hospital wards completed the curriculum (*Lancet* p. 186, Jan 18, 1896).

It was a small wonder that many early American physicians studied abroad. Edinburgh was popular because the language and customs most closely resembled that of the colonists and because the school was well-known and of sound reputation. John Fothergill, the benefactor of Pennsylvania Hospital and friend of William Shippen, Jr., was graduated from Edinburgh (Packard p. 143, 1933). Shippen's medical degree was also from Edinburgh. There was a need for organized medical education but the early medical schools in this country were little more than apprentice classes. The curriculum included materia medica, the study and preparation of drugs; physiology, the function of body structures; pathology, the observable anatomic changes resulting from disease processes; and anatomy and dissection, the detailed study of parts of the body and surgical correction of derangements of function. Anatomy was the most popular and important of the subjects. As medical schools developed so did the regulations and requirements for a doctor of medicine degree. There was no distinction between physician and surgeon and all students chose from the same basic subjects: Theory and Practice of Medicine, Anatomy, Materia Medica and Pharmacy, Chemistry, Surgery, Obstetrics, Diseases of Women and Children, and Institutes of Medicine. Generally a medical education required five years to complete. The candidate was at least 21 years of age, of good moral character, had served at least two years and preferably three in an apprenticeship role with a practitioner, completed two courses at a medical college, and submitted a thesis. Schools also required a clinical course at an approved institution or hospital (*Public Ledger* 6 Sept 1841). The Medical Department of the University of Pennsylvania was affiliated with Pennsylvania Hospital for this part of the training. In addition, some schools required a course in practical anatomy. Medical students, and indeed the profession as a whole, did not always command the respect they do today. Medical students were usually looked upon as a somewhat disreputable crowd, certainly vulgar, possibly depraved, and very intemperate. The Yale College catalog of the period noted that "medical

Opposite: A group of medical students engaged in a dissection. Philadelphia, circa 1900. Photo courtesy of Samuel W. Berkheiser, M.D. His father, Arthur Jonathan Berkheiser, is third from the left, immediately under the light.

students, during their residence in the Institution, are subject to the same moral and religious restraints, as those of the Academical College." The necessity of making such a comment indicates the thinking of the time.

Anatomy courses were the basis if not the primary reason for establishing medical schools. Atwater notes, "It is hard to overemphasize the importance of anatomical dissection in changing the medical curriculum, or opposition to it in retarding improvement. An attempt to offer better instruction in anatomy was the motivating force behind most, if not all, the early American medical schools" (p. 352). Not many preceptors were qualified or skilled in the subject, so the apprentice student lacked firsthand anatomical knowledge. Even with the established medical curricula, private courses in anatomy were popular. Anatomy was the only subject that could be demonstrated and was generally divided into two facets: (1) lectures on organs and skeletal structure illustrated by models, drawings, or possibly cadavers and (2) "practical" anatomy or dissection. The teaching of anatomy in medical schools was an active/interactive demonstration rather than the usual didactic experience offered by the medical training programs. Human cadavers were necessary for classroom dissection. The "performing of an anatomy" was considered to be an essential of medical education and, in the majority of schools, was a requirement for graduation. When Oliver Wendell Holmes began the study of medicine in Boston, he remarked, "I have been going to Massachusetts General Hospital and slicing and slivering the carcasses of better men and women than I ever was myself or am like to be. It is a sin for a puny little fellow like me to mutilate one of your six-foot men as if he were sheep, but vive la science" (Lassek p. 206). A few schools conferred degrees without anatomy courses, but they stopped this practice by the mid–1850s.

Often medical schools permitted students to take the dissection portion of the educational requirement at a place of their choice, and as a result a number of independent anatomy schools flowered in the early 1800s. Many of these were taught by the faculty of medical schools. The Philadelphia School of Anatomy on College Avenue offered five lectures each week, four in surgery and one in surgical anatomy. The lecturer was D. Hayes Agnew, M.D. Classes were held in the evening so that they would not interfere with instruction at medical schools but the anatomy rooms were available from 8:00 a.m. to 10:00 p.m. Other legitimate independent anatomy schools in Philadelphia included the College Avenue Anatomical School of William S. Forbes, M.D.; the Philadelphia Anatomical Rooms of Jason Valentine O'Brien Lawrence, M.D., and John D. Godman, M.D.; the Philadelphia Association for Medical Instruction; The Medical Institute of Philadelphia; and the School of Medicine (Baatz; "Some account").

The technique of anatomical injection is mentioned in several of the descriptive circulars for anatomy courses. Shippen alludes to it in his diary.

Alexander Monro Primus published his formula for injection solution, but other anatomists were not nearly so forthcoming, jealously guarding their own methods. Injections were practiced in order to preserve the cadaver or to "set" parts of the specimen. At first, air and colored liquid was tried, but dissection destroyed the material the doctors were trying to preserve. Anatomists then began to experiment with different concoctions that would be injected in a liquid state and would later solidify to retain shape. The most popular formula was one of beeswax, tallow, resin, and turpentine. Colors were added to preserve a natural look. The problem was to achieve or maintain duct temperature high enough that the wax did not set before the infusion was complete. Usually vessels were injected with hot water before initiation of the procedure. During the prime of dissection in the early 1800s, the use of spirits for preservation was discovered and, with suitable colors, bodies retained their "lifelike" appearance. A preparation of mercury was used in the lymphatic system but these specimens have proved much less durable and relatively few survive today (Tompsett p. 108–109). It was popular to inject colored wax into organs removed from the body and to varnish the surfaces for long-term preservation. The Dutch painting *Boekelman, President of the Society of Surgeons showing a colleague, Six, a heart with Injected Arteries* mentioned in Chapter 1, has immortalized a heart and vessels saved in such a manner. John Collins Warren, M.D., may have been the first American to attempt to preserve cadavers by embalming. His recipe was rum, arsenic and corrosive sublimate. The formula worked admirably. It is said that Warren kept a body for eight years in remarkably well-preserved condition.

Knowledge of anatomy was considered a prerequisite to achieve proficiency in surgery, and surgeons were held responsible for malpractice resulting from ignorance of anatomy. In his introductory lecture on the course in surgery at King's College, Dr. John Jones notes that the future surgeon "must possess an accurate knowledge of the human body acquir'd not only by attending anatomical lectures, but by frequently dissecting dead bodies with his own hands.... This practice can not be too warmly recommended to the students in surgery" (McDaniel). Samuel David Gross, M.D., taught operative surgery on cadavers. The following passage from Memoirs of John Abernethy illustrates the dilemma facing early practitioners. "Any surgeon who was convicted of mala praxis, resulting from ignorance of anatomy, was severely fined, perhaps ruined; and yet so entirely unprovided were the profession with any legitimate means of studying anatomy, that they could only be obtained by a connivance at practices the most demoralizing and revolting." Lonsdale commented that the English wished the medical profession to achieve standards of excellence but failed to take the steps needed to facilitate the acquisition of knowledge. "Every intelligent person knew that, as the rule and the square were to the architect and builder, and the compass to the sailor, so was anatomy to the surgeon; yet the means for its practice had to be obtained furtively, with that rare exception, the carrying out what might be designated the final *in terrorem* of the law against malefactors" (p. 59). "The law virtually proclaimed that the surgeon should possess aptitude and powers as well as a formal license to practise; nay, it went further, and subjected him who failed to display 'proper skill' to pecuniary forfeiture in the civil courts at the instigation of any dissatisfied patient; yet the only mode of acquiring that skill, namely, from dissections of the dead clandestinely obtained, was in the criminal court held to be a misdemeanor, punishable by fine and imprisonment!" (p. 62)

An editorial in the *Lancet* on January 25th, 1824, probably written by Thomas Wakley, M.D., addresses the problem posed by the law.

> If a surgeon commit an error in the practice of his profession, from a deficient knowledge of anatomy, by the common law of the land, the patient or sufferer may recover heavy damages; and it must be in the recollection of many of our readers, that a surgeon of this metropolis [London], named Pettigrew, had a verdict of 700 pounds awarded against him, for having mistaken a dislocation of the shoulder for a mere sprain. Of that verdict we do not complain. It is perfectly right to visit such gross ignorance with severe punishment; but what we do complain of is — the ridiculous anomaly of first making laws to punish medical practitioners if they do not possess a knowledge of their profession, and subsequently passing other laws which deprive them of the only source from whence it is possible that knowledge can be obtained.
>
> If dead bodies can not be procured, it will be impossible for the pupils to learn anatomy, and without anatomy, neither surgeons nor physicians can practice with the least prospect of benefiting their patients.

Pennsylvanian Thomas S. Sozinsky (p. 213) laments that medical men were made criminals in their attempts to acquire the knowledge that was legally demanded of them. Practicing on cadavers was certainly far preferable to turning hundreds of students out to ply their trade on live patients.

Knowledge gained by the study of normal and abnormal anatomy allowed established physicians to become more skilled in their diagnostic techniques. When the necessity for legal post mortems arose, physicians who were exposed to practical anatomy were much better prepared to determine the cause of death than practitioners who never had been. In addition, dissections provided the raw material for the original descriptions of many diseases.

William Shippen, Jr's, contribution to American medicine in the field of anatomy is a milestone. He recognized the need for a solid foundation of medical knowledge gained through experience in dissection and put his ideas into practice by becoming the first professor of anatomy in Colonial America. His educational credentials for this endeavor were impeccable and his social standing in Philadelphia helped his effort.

William Shippen, Jr., M.D.,
The First American Professor of Anatomy

William Shippen, the younger, was one of the greatest medical teachers in 18th century America. The son and namesake of a respected Philadelphia physician, Shippen was born October 21, 1736. He received his preliminary education under the direction of Dr. Samuel Finley, a Presbyterian clergyman, at West Nottingham in Chester County, Pennsylvania. He was graduated from the College of New Jersey (Princeton) in 1754, the valedictorian of his class. He returned to Philadelphia to study medicine as an apprentice to his father for four years before traveling to Europe to study in London, France, and Edinburgh.

While in London, Shippen attended lectures in anatomy given by John Hunter, and midwifery, by William Hunter and Dr. Colin Mackenzie. A portion of Shippen's diary, the only written record in his own hand that has survived to the present, is a description of his days at Hunter's anatomy school and his activities there. The course in anatomy consisted of dissecting throughout the day, followed by a lecture from five o'clock to approximately seven thirty. Teaching continued through weekends as well. William Hunter supplied each of his students with one whole body to dissect. These were usually secured through the legal pathways. Hunter, mindful of the public opinion regarding the dead, cautioned his classes not to speak of the activities in the laboratory and not to show the rooms to strangers. Cadavers were also used to perfect the art of surgery and injection and Shippen mentions injections several times in his diary.

London was also where Shippen made the acquaintance of Dr. John Fothergill, a kindly Quaker. From him Shippen received the gift of the Fothergill casts and drawings, a series of anatomical studies of the human body. The collection comprised 18 crayon drawings by van Rymsdyck, three cases of anatomical models by Jenty, and one skeleton (Middelton: Shippen [I] p. 443). There is some speculation that the van Rymsdyck drawings were discards from the collection that would eventually make up William Hunter's *Anatomy of the Gravid Uterus* (1774). Fothergill's donation to Pennsylvania Hospital, valued at 350 pounds, was accompanied by a letter in which he wrote, "In want of real subjects, these will have their use and I have recommended to Dr. Shippen to give a course of anatomical lectures to such as may attend; he is well qualified for the subject...." (Norris p.126). Having earned his medical degree from Edinburgh in 1761, Shippen returned to the United States and, in 1762, began his first lectures on anatomy in Philadelphia, the announcement of which appeared in the *Pennsylvania Gazette*.

Philadelphia, November 11th, 1762

Mr. Hall, Sir,
Please to inform the public that a course of anatomical lectures will be opened this winter in Philadelphia, for the advantage of the young gentlemen now engaged in the study of Physic, in this and the neighboring provinces whose circumstances and connections will not admit of their going abroad for improvement to the anatomical schools of Europe; and also for the entertainment of any gentlemen who may have the curiosity to understand the anatomy of the Human Frame. In these lectures the situation, figure and structure of all the parts of the human body will be demonstrated, their respective uses explained, and as far as a course of anatomy will permit, their diseases, with the indications and methods of cure briefly treated of;
All the necessary operations in surgery will be performed, a course of bandages exhibited, and the whole conclude with an explanation of some of the curious phenomena that arise from an examination of the gravid uterus, and a few plain general directions in the study and practice of midwifery. The necessity and public utility of such a course in this growing country, and the method to be pursued therein, will be more particularly explained in an Introductory Lecture, to be delivered the 16th instant, at six o'clock in the evening, at the State House, by William Shippen, Jun./ M.D.

The lectures were given at his father's house on Fourth Street. Because the public was opposed to anatomical dissection, the house was stoned several times, windows smashed and, at least once, Dr. Shippen was forced to make his escape through a private alley. This prompted his public denial through letters to local newspapers of any wrongdoing or illegal acquisition of cadavers. The *Pennsylvania Gazette* on September 26, 1765, carried an announcement of anatomical lectures to be given and included a disclaimer penned by Dr. Shippen.

Dr. Shippen's course of anatomical lectures will begin on Thursday, the 14th of November, 1765; it will consist of about 60 lectures, in which the situation, figure, and structure of all the parts of the human body will be demonstrated on the fresh subject; their respective uses explained and their diseases; with the indications and method of cure, briefly treated of; all the necessary operations in surgery will be performed, a course on bandages given; and the whole conclude with a few plain and general directions in the practice of midwifery. Each person to pay five pistoles.
Those who incline to attend the Pennsylvania Hospital and have the benefit of the curious anatomical plates and casts there, to pay six pistoles to that useful charity.

MASTER
READING
the Art of

It has given Dr. Shippen much Pain to hear that notwithstanding all the Caution and Care he has taken to preserve the utmost decency in opening and dissecting dead Bodies, which he has persevered in chiefly from the Motive of being useful to Mankind, some evil-minded persons, either wantonly or maliciously, have reported to his Disadvantage that he has taken up some persons who were buried in the Church Burying Ground, which has disturbed the Minds of some of his worthy Fellow Citizens. The Doctor, with much Pleasure, improves this Opportunity to declare that the Report is absolutely false; and to assure them that the Bodies he dissected were either of Persons who had wilfully murdered themselves or were publicly executed, except now and then one from the Potter's Field, whose Death was owing to some particular Disease; and that he never had one Body from the Church or any other private burial place.

In January 11, 1770, Dr. Shippen again addressed his Philadelphia neighbors on the practice of body snatching through the pages of the *Pennsylvania Gazette*.

To the Public.
Many of the Inhabitants of this City, I hear, have been much terrified by sundry wicked and malicious Reports, of my taking up Bodies from the several Burying-grounds in this Place; notwithstanding these Fears are groundless, the Reports false, and seem either made and propagated by weak and prejudiced Persons, or intended to injure my Character, yet Humanity obliges me to suppress all Feelings of Resentment and Contempt, and do all in my Power to remove these, tho' groundless, Fears; which I do, by declaring, in the most solemn Manner, that I never have had, and that I never will have, directly or indirectly, one Subject from the Burying-ground belonging to any Denomination of Christians whatever; Having been informed that two families were very lately much terrified by unkind insinuations, that their deceased Friends would not rest in their Graves, I waited on them, with a sincere desire to relieve their distressed Minds, and made no Doubt but I should receive such Information from them, as would enable me to trace these black stories to their blacker Original; but after much diligent inquiry, not one Author could be found, and all, Yes!, all these terrible fears, all this Belief of those wicked and foolish, nay, almost impossible stories, depended, as a Gentleman sensibly expressed it himself, on [mere false charges (?)]; all the Information I could get was, that it was generally believed I had taken up a young Lady from Christ-Church Burying-ground, whose Grave has been opened within these few Days, and her Body found in its sacred Repository undisturbed. And secondly, that scarce any one doubted but I had in my Theatre the Body of Elizabeth Roberts, who formerly lived as Housekeeper with William Lyons, Esq; this Woman, as Dr. Kearsley jun. (who attended her in her last illness) has given me from under his Hand, died in the Middle of Summer of a putrid Fever, yet no one doubts but I dissected her in the middle of Winter....I have persevered in teaching this difficult and most useful branch of medical knowledge, tho' attended with very disagreeable circumstances, chiefly from the Motive of public Good, and have, and always will preserve the utmost Decency, with regard to

the Dead; and do solemnly protest, that none of your House, or Kindred, shall ever be disturbed in their silent Graves, by me, or any under my Care. And it has been also asserted, that Subjects might have been brought from those Burial Places by my pupils, without my knowledge, I have added an Affidavit of Joseph Harrison, student of medicine, who has lived in my Father's House ever since I began my anatomical lectures, and who has had an Opportunity of knowing where every Body was obtained, that ever I dissected in America.

W. Shippen, Jun, Professor of Anatomy

In 1765, the College of Philadelphia established a medical department where Shippen became the professor of anatomy and surgery while John Morgan was professor of medicine. The Revolutionary War interrupted medical studies and Dr. Shippen served as the Director-General of the Military Hospital and Physician-In-Chief of the Continental Army until 1781. A series of disagreements with John Morgan over the administration of the military hospital system and procurement of supplies caused enmity between these two men which lasted long after the war and spilled over into their professional and personal lives. The details of the Morgan-Shippen feud are found in Middleton's paper on the life of William Shippen, Jr.

The anatomical lectures resumed in 1779 in the newly created Medical Department of the University of the State of Pennsylvania. In 1791, the College of Philadelphia and the University of the State of Pennsylvania joined under the name of University of Pennsylvania where Shippen assumed the chair in anatomy, surgery, and midwifery.

Shippen has been described by a number of his contemporaries. Following is a picture from the pen of Caspar Wistar, M.D., professor of anatomy at the University of Pennsylvania.

> Nature had been uncommonly bountiful in his form and endowments. His person was graceful, his manners polished, his conversation various, and the tones of his voice singularly sweet and conciliatory. In his intercourse with society he was gay without levity, and dignified without haughtiness or austerity. He belonged to a family, proverbial for good temper. His father, whom he strongly resembled in this respect, during the long life of ninety years, had scarcely ever been seen out of humour. He was also particularly agreeable to young people. Known as he was to almost every citizen of Philadelphia, it is probable that there was no one who did not wish him well. This portrait is strongly coloured, but there are yet many amongst us who remember the original, and to them I appeal for its truth [Eulogium p. 177].

Shippen married Alice Lee, the daughter of Thomas Lee of Virginia, in 1760 while he was still studying in Edinburgh. They had eight children but only two survived. Shippen was apparently not the paragon at home that he appeared to be in professional life. His only surviving daughter

Nancy, at the age of 18, attracted many suitors to the household. Among them were Bushrod Washington, a nephew of George Washington; Louis Otto, a young French diplomat; and Colonel Henry Livingston, a wealthy middle-aged New Yorker. Nancy chose Otto but was forced by her father to wed Livingston because of the potential wealth he offered the family. Even though her marriage was miserable, young Nancy remained with Livingston nearly two years before she returned home with her infant daughter. When she sued her husband for divorce, Shippen sided with Livingston. Lest the inheritance which Shippen coveted be lost, he sent the little girl to live with her father, an act which caused Alice Shippen to have a nervous breakdown. Nancy's mental state deteriorated too. By the time the child was old enough to flee Livingston and return to her mother, the damage to the Shippen family had been done. Nancy Shippen Livingston had become a religious fanatic as did her daughter, who did eventually inherit her father's fortune but, alas, too late. She died a spinster and a recluse at the age of 82 in 1864, a tribute to her grandfather's selfishness.

While Nancy and her mother were reduced to various states of mental derangement, Shippen's only surviving son, Thomas Lee Shippen, spent six years dying of tuberculosis. His death was a great blow to William. He all but retired from medical practice and teaching for nearly a decade.

In 1805, Shippen resumed his medical activities. One of the founders of the College of Physicians of Philadelphia, he was elected as its second president succeeding John Redman, M.D., and served until 1808. He died of a wasting disease brought on by anthrax on July 11, 1808, at his summer home in Germantown. The wasting disease may well have been diabetes (Corner p. 124; Hartwell; Kelly and Burrage p. 1104–1106; Norwood; Middleton, parts 1 & 2). One of his old adversaries, Benjamin Rush, attended him during his last illness. Although Rush was outwardly gracious, he penned the following remarks about Shippen in his diary. "He had talents, but which from disease became weak. He was too indolent to write, to read, and even to think, but with the stock of knowledge he acquired when young maintained some rank in his profession especially as a teacher of anatomy in which he was eloquent, luminous and pleasing ... His chief pleasures consisted in the enjoyments of the table" (Flexner p. 87–89). Perhaps Rush's comments were not made in rancor but in truth. None of Shippen's lecture notes survive today, if he had any. He wrote nothing except his doctoral dissertation and a regrettably short diary of his Edinburgh experience. What little is known of his anatomy courses has been learned from the notes his students took from his lectures. These indicate that he brought from Europe the state of the art in anatomy at the time, and thus made a very great contribution to American medical education.

Grave, n. A place in which the dead are laid to await the coming of the medical student.
— Ambrose Bierce:
The Devil's Dictionary

RESURRECTION OF THE DEAD

Acquiring Bodies

The ploys for acquiring bodies before burial required considerable imagination and theatrics or a substantial exchequer. Some claimants for the dead came from impostors in the guise of mourning kin and are exemplified by Merry Andrew and his crew. Outright bribery or purchase of bodies from undertakers or church sextons was practiced by those students and physicians with sufficient financial means. Battlefields strewn with unidentified and unclaimed dead soldiers gave some anatomists a wealth of material with which to work. John Warren, M.D., of Boston, a Revolutionary War physician, wrote of his virtually unlimited supply of corpses from the New York-New Jersey campaign.

Acquisition of unclaimed dead by resurrectionists in the guise of "mourning relatives" is related by Lonsdale in vivid detail. "Marvelous were the expedients resorted to by these false claimants of the unprotected dead, and equally marvelous was their success, considering that all the various personifications of character rested with so small a group as three or four men, one of whom had to profess direct kinsmanship with the deceased" (p. 103–105).

Andrew Lees or Merrilees, also known as Merry Andrew, was apparently quite an actor. Merry Andrew was a tall, thin character who flapped about as though he had St. Vitus dance (Cole p. 104). In his role as mourner, he was able to transform his face to fit the solemnity of the occasion and became suffused with tears when discussing his "deceased" relative. He made the initial contact early in the day and returned later with friends, including a mock minister, to remove the remains to the family

26

burial place in the country. His friends, the Spoon and Moldewarp (the Mole) by name, acquired their pseudonyms from the services at which they excelled. The Spoon was skilled at scooping of bodies from coffins while the Mole was a furious digger. Spoon also doubled as a preacher (Cole p. 104). Typical of all resurrection men, each could perform all of the tasks necessary for a successful venture. A "burial service" was sometimes held before the small funeral cortege proceeded on its way. As soon as the group was quite clear of detection, either by distance or by darkness, the body was transferred with all possible haste to the anatomical rooms. The "mourners" then retired, with cash in hand, to the nearest pub for a night of debauchery.

It is said that Merry Andrew had the keenest wit of the three. Spoon and Mole were at pains to best Andrew at their macabre game. Having heard of the death of Andrew's sister and the place of burial, the two resurrectionists repaired to the cemetery to claim her. They succeeded in locating and uncovering the coffin. The lid was removed and they were about to lift the corpse when a ghost arose from behind a nearby tombstone terrifying Spoon and Mole. They deserted the cemetery leaving both the corpse and the ghost to their own designs. Merry Andrew, who was of course the specter, finished the job his two traitorous colleagues had begun and resurrected his sister. He supposedly secreted her body in a cellar from whence he later recovered her and sold her to the surgeons (Cole p. 104–105).

Since it required less physical labor to obtain a body before burial, the more ingenious and wealthy of the body snatchers might bribe an undertaker or grave digger to bury an empty albeit weighted coffin. After the family and friends had departed, the body was sacked up for transport, possibly for immediate removal, but often buried in a shallow grave to facilitate recovery after dark.

Impostors were also used to claim bodies of those who died in almshouses. The "bereaved" relatives arrived in mourning clothes and took possession of a cadaver, either convincing the guardian of their authenticity or paying him to look the other way. In an investigation in 1856 at the Philadelphia Almshouse of allegations that "a member of this Board . . . prostitut[ed] his office to his own personal profit in making merchandise of the bodies of deceased paupers," it was discovered that a discrepancy of 21 bodies existed. The investigating committee reported, "These gentlemen went on to show that no account was kept at the graveyard of the number of burials, and the only records were the small pieces of paper tacked on the heads of the coffins, on which the names, etc., were written, and are liable to be removed from various causes before the coffins reach the graveyard. . . . Such notices have been found and frequently picked up on the the grounds of the institution." The report recommended that the house agent be furnished with books in which to maintain records. The newspapers alleged a cover-up and suggested that a Dr. E.B. Mosely, member of the Board at the Almshouse, was connected with the sale of bodies. The Board acquired the unlovely epithet of "Board of Buzzards" (Lawrence p. 207–208).

Professional medical rivalry for bodies of interesting cases from the Almshouse existed as illustrated by the following report to the Board.

> Dr. Smith, the Chief Medical Officer, admitted that he had preserved two dead bodies for the purpose of obtaining two rare specimens of diseases, and claimed that by so doing, he was only in the pursuit of a legitimate and proper privilege, one which he had a perfect right to exercise for the advancement of medical science.
>
> The evidence showed that Dr. Kelly, one of the assistant physicians, was anxious to obtain the fractured arms of a female who had died of consumption. Dr. Smith was equally anxious to obtain them as valuable specimens of morbid anatomy. After Dr. Smith's trouble in preparing the body to prevent decomposition, some other physician, outside of the institution, procured them. The disappointment of Dr. Kelly was to a great extent the origin of this investigation, and the result of it proves absolutely nothing.

Lawrence's pithy comment on this Board report bears repeating. He wrote, "This was indeed a wonderful report. It showed the great care that was taken of the bodies. It was certainly too bad that Dr. Kelly should be disappointed, especially when he was so anxious; but there was Dr. Smith, who had taken the trouble to preserve it, and then to think that 'some other physician outside of the institution procured them!' Who was this other physician, and how did he procure them? The committee failed to state whether this 'other physician' took them out secreted in his vest pocket, or how he did take them. Possibly the body walked out" (p. 215).

The Ferryman, Purveyor of Human Flesh

At the Philadelphia Almshouse, there existed an individual known simply as the ferryman. He was described as having the appearance of a ghoul. Among the tasks assigned to this person was to "attend to the duties of the graveyard," which he apparently did with great efficiency and personal profit. Since medical students required human bodies for anatomic education and the public was generally unaware of the Almshouse cemetery, corpses of those individuals not claimed by friends were sold to the colleges with impunity. The revenue accrued from this operation was appropriated by the ferryman. None of the profit was paid to the Almshouse. Mr. Linnard of the Board of Guardians drew attention to the brisk trade in body snatching. He objected "to this traffic in human corpses, and especially when the proceeds do not inure to the benefit of the city." Mr. Linnard felt that the profit from the sale of bodies should have been applied against the expense of caring for a veritable army of paupers. He made an attempt to remove the ferryman to curtail this modern practice of body snatching at the Almshouse. How successful he was in his campaign was not reported (Lawrence p. 252–253).

John Warren, M.D.

John Warren, Revolutionary War physician, was charged with the operation of the Continental Army Hospital in Boston in 1777–1782 and before that functioned as a hospital surgeon during the siege of Boston and the New York–New Jersey campaign of 1775–1777. Dr. Warren was an anatomist, the first professor of anatomy at Harvard Medical School, and may have been a member of a secret anatomical society, The Spunkers, during his undergraduate years there. His army connections enabled him to "procure a multitude of subjects from having access to the bodies of soldiers who had died without relations." After the war, it was considerably more difficult to acquire the raw material for anatomical demonstrations. "Bodies of executed criminals were occasionally procured; and sometimes a pauper subject was obtained, averaging not more than two a year" (Warren p. 404).

In 1806, John Collins Warren, the son of John Warren, opened a dissecting room on Marlborough Street in Boston. Students attending the school obtained the bodies necessary for study and, in the early years at least, there was no dearth of material. However, as medical programs proliferated in New England, the market for anatomical specimens grew. It became vastly more difficult to keep the supply of bodies on hand. Students from the developing schools were sent to Boston to procure subjects, which they did in a very careless and sloppy manner. The public, thus aroused by blatant grave robbing, set grave watchers in the burial yards. The students from Boston were forced to look to New York for cadavers, a dangerous and expensive alternative to the quiet, peaceful operation they had conducted before competition became rampant. Several times their agents were arrested, tried, and fined for their illegal procurement business. "At that time, scarcely any exhumation occurred without some similar accidents of the most disagreeable and sometimes painful character. The record of them would make a black-book, which, though the odium of it should belong to few individuals, would do no credit to the enlightenment of Boston in the nineteenth century, and convey an idea of the state of feeling of a professor of anatomy on the approach and during the course of his anatomical pursuits" (Warren p. 409).

John Collins Warren, M.D., Ventures Into Body Snatching

John Collins Warren began his adventures in body snatching when he was still in college. His first person account reveals the excitement he must have felt; his father's response betrays the fearful danger that accompanied such exploits.

While in college, I began the business of getting subjects in 1796. Having understood that a man without relations was to be buried in the North Burying-ground, I formed a party, of which Dr. William Ingalls was one. He was a physician of Boston at that time. We reached the spot at ten o'clock at night. The night was rather light. We soon found the grave; but, after proceeding a while, were led to suspect a mistake and went on to another place. Here we found ourselves wrong and returned to the first; and, having set watches, we proceeded rapidly, uncovering the coffin by breaking it open. We took out the body of a stout young man, put it in a bag, and carried it to the burying-ground wall. As we were going to lift it over and put it in the chaise, we saw a man walking along the edge of the wall outside, smoking. A part of us disappeared. One of the company met him, stopped him from coming on, and entered into conversation with him. This individual of our party affected to be intoxicated, while he contrived to get into a quarrel with the stranger. After he had succeeded in doing this, another of the party, approaching, pretended to side with the stranger, and ordered the other to go about his business. Taking the stranger by the arm, he led him off in a different direction to some distance; then left him, and returned to the burying-ground. The body was then quickly taken up, and packed in the chaise between two of the parties, who drove off to Cambridge with their booty. Two of us staid to fill the grave; but my companion, being alarmed, soon left the burying-ground; and I knowing the importance of covering up the grave and effacing the vestiges of our labor, remained, with no very agreeable sensations, to finish the work. However, I got off without further interruption; drove, with the tools, to Cambridge; and arrived just before daylight. When my father came up in the morning to lecture, and found that I had been engaged in this scrape, he was very much alarmed; but when the body was uncovered, and he saw what a fine healthy subject it was, he seemed to be as much pleased as I ever saw him. This body lasted the course through.

Dr. Warren's preservation methods must have been excellent for the normal length of time to complete the "anatomizing" of a corpse was between seven and ten days. Longer than that, the body became too decomposed to be useful for study. Dissection was done in haste for search and seizure by the local constabulary were common occurrences.

Later in his career when Dr. Warren was instructing medical students, he requested two young men to obtain a subject for dissection. These gentlemen watched as an Almshouse resident was buried, taking care to mark the grave so that it could later be found. The watch schedule for the

cemetery was determined and sometime after midnight, disinterment occurred. While one student remained in the vicinity, the other went to secure
the transportation for which he had earlier arranged. The wagon was
drawn up to the burial ground to receive the body when the watchmen
sprang upon the two students. One jumped on the wagon and departed
dragging several of the watchmen along after him. Once rid of these men,
the student drove about until morning and returned to town with an air of
innocence. The other student was not so fortunate. He was seized and was
being escorted to the watch-house when he made his escape through a
marshy drainage area. Having ascertained that he was free of danger, he
ascended from the ditch and walked boldly up the street whereupon he was
again captured. He escaped a second time and managed to hide himself
under a pile of fine shavings where he fell asleep. Warren avers that the
strenuous pursuit which the young man endured resulted in hemorrhage
from the lungs leading to consumption and premature death. "When we
consider that this fine young man fell victim to narrow-minded prejudices,
we involuntarily ask whether we had gone back to the time of superstition
and witchcraft" (E. Warren p. 409).

Dr. Warren related yet another tale of a medical student whom he was
privileged to know. This student had a flair for procuring bodies and frequently worked alone. He had carefully scouted the South Burial-ground
in Boston and marked a grave to be opened. When he returned to the
cemetery that night, he was surprised by a party of watchmen who arrested
him. He appeared for court the following morning charged with being in
the burial ground for the purpose of digging up bodies. The student met the
charges with great indignation and countered that the watchmen were con-
spiring to extort money from him and impugn his excellent reputation. In
the face of his fierce attack — and the total lack of evidence — he was freed
and the accusations dropped. Warren notes that the man was graduated
with a medical degree and set up a practice in the city of Mexico (E. Warren
p. 411).

A Resurrection Handbook

The actual method of disinterment of bodies provides entertaining, if
somewhat gruesome, reading. Many reputed authorities have written with
considerable detail the technique of removing a corpse from the coffin. The
accounts of Cheyne, Cooper, Christison, and Wakley differ in style and
pattern, but most body snatchers agreed that early evenings during the late
fall and early winter months were ideal for removal of the prize. The type
of cemetery made a difference in susceptibility to the attentions of grave
robbers, with Potter's Fields ranking high among those raided most often.

Bodies in black cemeteries were less safe than those in other private or church-affiliated burial grounds. Although cadaver-producing contracts between individual professional body snatchers and medical schools have not been discovered with great frequency, a few did exist as exemplified by Dr. S.E. French. His shipment methods seem to have been faulty and instructions from an·experienced physician/anatomist give a glimpse at the practical aspects of traffic in human remains.

In 1818, Dr. John Cheyne (of Cheyne-Stokes respiration fame) wrote of body snatching in Dublin for the School of Medicine. His remarks were in a letter that he wrote to Dr. Edward Percival. Following is a portion of the text of that letter.

> The bodies used most in dissecting rooms are derived from the great cemetery for the poor called the Hospital Fields — vulgo Bullys Acre; these, there being no regular resurrection men, are procured by the pupils who, fixing upon a grave, are influenced by the appearance of fresh earth, scattered around it, by the freshness of the sods if there are any, and by the looseness of the substratum of soil, which is probed by a pointed instrument called "a poker." But notwithstanding great enterprize and exertion and disregard of danger which sometimes is also great, the work being done by amateurs, and not be regular members of this part of the profession, disappointments ensued, and the subjects raised were often in an advanced stage of putrefaction and certainly the dissecting rooms are often supplied with bodies which have been under ground for a fortnight or three weeks. In the work of exhumation the upper part of the grave is cleared, the corresponding part of the lid of the coffin is torn up, and then by means of a noose round its neck the body is extracted by main force. The bodies tied up in a sack, neck and heels, are subject of great violence, during their transport from the Burying ground — as for example, they are dropt from a high wall, by which it is well known fractures of the cervical vertebra not infrequently occur. To conclude, the cadaver is roughly handled in the dissecting room, being often left with the head hanging over the table, by which means the blood gravitates and congestion of the brain to a great extent is the consequence [British Medical Journal 1:74, January 16, 1943].

Most of us have the mistaken impression, probably from some of the popular literature on body snatching such as Robert Louis Stevenson's *The Body Snatcher*, that to disinter a body, the coffin must be completely uncovered and raised from the ground. Such is not the case, and no self-respecting grave robber would have loitered in a cemetery for the length of time it would have taken to accomplish this task. Montgomery notes that graves were opened by locating the direction of the head, removing the earth in a vertical tunnel with a wooden spade, removing the head of the roughbox, hooking the body, and then replacing the earth. It was relatively simple to determine the location of the head since, in Christian burial grounds, the body was placed with the feet facing east. If it was an established cemetery, the direction of the tombstones provided the information. Sir Astley Cooper raises the following objections to this method. The body snatcher would be working in old, instead of soft new ground and because the grave would be lengthened, the resurrection would be detected at once. In addition, he notes that the head of the coffin is the narrowest part and egress of the chest and shoulders of the corpse would have been difficult (p. 354–355). Sir Astley's version is that one-third of the coffin was unearthed. A specially designed crowbar was inserted under the lid to lever it off. The lid usually snapped at about the area where the weight of the earth pressed on the still-interred two-thirds of the coffin. The only difficulty, notes Sir Astley, was when the lid failed to move, but "...this, however, scarcely ever occurred in the coffins of the poorer classes, to which the operations of the Resurrectionists were usually directed" (p. 350–351).

Sir Robert Christison's account agrees closely with that of Sir Astley.

> A hole was dug down to the coffin only where the head lay — a canvas sheet being stretched around to receive the earth and to prevent any of it spoiling the smooth uniformity of the grass. The digging was done with short, flat, dagger-shaped implements of wood, to avoid the clicking noise of iron striking stones. On reaching the coffin, two broad iron hooks under the lid, pulled forcibly up with a rope, broke off a sufficient portion of the lid to allow the body to be dragged out; and sacking was heaped over the whole to deaden the sound of the cracking wood. The body was stripped of the graveclothes, which were scrupulously buried again; it was secured in a sack; and the surface of the ground was carefully restored to its original condition, — which was difficult, as the sod over a fresh-filled grave must always present signs of recent disturbance. The whole process could be completed in an hour, even though the grave might be six feet deep, because the soil was loose, and the digging was done impetuously by frequent relays of active men [p. 176].

It appears that the only time a coffin was completely uncovered was where several burials occurred in the same grave. In this case, several cadavers might be recovered with minimal effort by raising each coffin in succession (Cooper p. 351).

Thomas Wakley's biography in the *Lancet* January 18, 1896, addresses the method of body snatching.

> Special tools were wanted: sharp curved spades on long handles, scoops on jointed shafts, grappling forceps, files and light crowbars. The impression that nothing could be easier than to go to a churchyard and dig out a newly filled grave, break open the coffin, and make off with the unpleasant booty in a sack is erroneous. This might have been practicable

where the earth was loosly piled in and very untidy, but a neatly finished grave would very soon give evidence if it had been tampered with. In the case of a neat or not quite new grave the ingenuity of the resurrectionist came into play. Several feet — FIFTEEN OR TWENTY — away from the head or foot of the grave he would remove a square of turf about eighteen or twenty inches in diameter. This he would carefully put by, and then commence to mine. Most pauper graves were of the same depth, and if the sepulchre was that of a person of importance the depth of the grave could be pretty well estimated by the nature of the soil thrown up. Taking a five foot grave, the coffin lid would be about four feet from the surface. A rough slanting tunnel SOME FIVE YARDS LONG would therefore, have to be constructed so as to impinge exactly on the coffin head. This being at last struck (no very simple task), the coffin was lugged up by hooks to the surface, or, preferably, the end of the coffin wrenched off with hooks while still in the shelter of the tunnel, and the scalp or feet of the corpse secured through the open end and the body pulled out, leaving the coffin almost intact and unmoved. The body once obtained, the narrow shaft was easily filled up and the sod of turf accurately replaced. The friends of the deceased, seeing that the earth over his grave was not disturbed, would flatter themselves that the body had escaped the resurrectionist; but they seldom noticed the square of turf some feet away.

Wakley's version of a successful snatch is even more unbelievable than that of raising the entire coffin and body snatchers rarely opened a "not quite new grave." Special tools such as jointed scoops were not commonly the tools of grave robbers. Fifteen or twenty feet of mining through unturned soil would undoubtedly have been more than one night's work even for the most energetic resurrectionist. Pulling the coffin out through this 18- or 20-inch diameter tunnel borders on the ridiculous; friction alone would have made the task nearly impossible. Extracting the body through the head portion of the coffin where it is narrowest encounters the same objections voiced by Sir Astley Cooper. Crawling into an enclosed space to wrench off the head of the coffin where no leverage could have been applied would have required strength greater than Samson.

While much of the information in the Wakley biography on actual body snatching appears to be fictional, observations on the number of empty coffins in cemeteries probably are not. Since the members of the medical profession were the only benefactors where body snatching was concerned, it seems apparent that if they were not the perpetrators, then they were at least the instigators.

Since embalming was not a practice, bodies had to be disinterred promptly before an advanced state of decay rendered them impossible to use for the study of anatomy. Often resurrection occurred on the same day as the burial. The process was carried out after dark, preferably on moonless or cloudy nights. Sir Robert Christison writes:

The time chosen in the dark winter nights was, for the town church-yards, from six to eight o'clock; at which latter hour the churchyard watch was set, and the city police also commenced their night rounds.... Opera-tions in the country were necessarily conducted at a later hour. Certain country churchyards were selected for convenience of approach, and their distance from houses. Although there was more risk in such circum-stances, owing to the necessity of using a gig, and the inquiries that were apt to take place at toll-bars, no one was ever caught. But narrow escapes were sometimes made [p. 176–177].

Shaded lanterns were sometimes used and some grave robbers even erected a tent or lean-to over the area while they worked. This prevented passing citizens from spotting the light and raising the alarm. Time of year had little effect on disinterment other than the extreme heat of summer when decay occurred very quickly. Snow also limited grave robbing because, at daybreak, tracks were readily visible and advertised the nefarious ac-tivities. However, a snowstorm very effectively covered all evidence of dis-turbance in the cemetery. Rain made the situation much more difficult be-cause the loose ground turned to mud and became heavy and unwieldy.

Some cemeteries were more susceptible to the attentions of body snatch-ers than others. Cemeteries that were considered fair game for robbing were the paupers' graves, or "potter's fields." In November 1862, the Board of Guardians of the Philadelphia Almshouse in the person of Mr. Dickinson registered dismay at the disappearance of bodies by offering the following resolution. "That the steward be instructed to have the bodies of those who die in the House placed in the receiving vaults, there to remain as provided for by the rules of the Board." Mr. Dickinson did not seem to be nearly so upset about the use of the bodies as the illegal traffic. He noted that in New York, the colleges were entitled to bodies of paupers "and get them without pay; while here there is a regular traffic in dead bodies, which the Board is anxious to stop. This business has been going on all summer. As soon as the burying of bodies in the graveyard was begun, the colleges com-menced to steal them" (Lawrence p. 270). It was reported to the Board at this meeting that bodies were on the move every night and that "about three weeks ago a body was found lying near the fence on the grounds," a case of resurrection interrupted in the act.

In 1879 Sozinsky (p. 216–217) reported, "The number of bodies that are allowed to go into the potter's fields throughout the country is very small and the majority of those that reach them are not allowed to rest in them many hours. I am so positive of these assertions, that I do not consider it necessary to present any proof in support of them." William Shippen, Jr., admitted using bodies from potter's fields. Lawrence commented that, although it was written that friends and or relatives of patients who died in the Almshouse were to be contacted, in cases where no known friends could be found, no rules applied to the examination (dissection) of bodies. It was understood that examinations were not to be conducted any oftener than necessary and then with dignity and decency. Little heed was given the first injunction and utter disregard to the second. Members of the Board of the Almshouse unfortunately discovered remains "too revolting to be described" in an unoccupied part of the building and it appeared that the mutilated bodies had been there for several months (p. 159).

P.T. Barnum's Cannibal

A cannibal who was exhibited in P.T. Barnum's circus succumbed, it is said, to the vicissitudes of the average diet of central Pennsylvanians and was buried in old Potter's Field in York County. The York City Council voted in 1897 to sell the cemetery and move the bodies, an estimated five hundred or so. On April 7, 1897, the York *Dispatch* reported that the body of the cannibal was not found among the remains, thus establishing the truth of the story that the body had been snatched. None of the jewelry that adorned the man when he was interred remained and the only evidence of his occupancy was the lone coffin lid. Rumor was that a York physician removed the corpse, dissected the remains, boiled the bones, and then assembled the skeleton which graced his office (Hubley p. 15–17).

Private cemeteries, such as family burial plots, in rural areas were choice targets for body snatchers. They were usually located some distance from inhabited dwellings where discovery of a night's labor was unlikely. City church burial yards were usually left untouched because raids were more easily detected owing to the closely populated areas in which they were located. Rural cemeteries were isolated by comparison. It is thought-provoking that medical schools in rural areas claimed to acquire their cadavers from the city, while city schools claimed their anatomic material came from the country.

Desecration at St. Mary's Church

The following report of grave robbery appeared in the local affairs column of the *Public Ledger*, September 26, 1841.

On Friday night last, the graveyard of St. Mary's Church, in Hamilton Village, was entered by some villains, and the body of Mr. William Davis, one of the oldest citizens of that village, who died on the 20th inst., was disinterred and carried off for the purpose of dissection. The outrage was discovered early Saturday morning, and application was made to Henry Leech, Esq, who instituted a search, which resulted in the recovery of the body from a private dissecting house, and its restoration to the distressed relatives of the deceased. Such was the haste in which this act appears to have been perpetrated, that there was not time taken to fill up the grave after the disinterment, and fragments of the coffin were strewed about as if it had been rudely broken to pieces, in order to get at and secrete the body. Lest injustice should be done, by imputing this outrage to innocent parties, we are authorized to say that it was not known of, or sanctioned by the faculty of either of the medical schools in this city; nor by the owner of the establishment where the body was found, he being absent from the city at the time.

Northerners claimed their cadavers came from the South. Some evidence supports this premise. In "a letter addressed to the dean of the medical school at Bowdoin College (Maine) from the dean here [Medical School of Maryland] in response to a question about whether he (the Maryland dean) could supply cadavers [,] it gave a price and method of shipment, in whiskey barrels..." (Cohen)

Ohio newspapers investigating the procurement of bodies at Ohio Medical College uncovered so-called "cadaver-producing contracts," agreements between one or more medical colleges and the resurrectionists to supply sufficient material for anatomical demonstration. "Pickles" was the label most often attached to casks in which bodies were shipped (Kelly p. 197). The means was a distribution system that was centered in Cincinnati and culminated in many smaller cities (Sievers). The Harrison resurrection story (detailed later) contains a reference to wholesale shipment of bodies. The post mortem travels of Augustus Devin lend credence to the allegations.

Post–Civil War Washington, D.C., also served as a base of shipping operations for cadaver procurement activities. When George Christian was arrested on December 13, 1873, for digging up dead bodies and disposing of them for profit, he carried, in addition to other interesting items, two letters. These exposed a part of his business and at least two of his contacts. They also reveal that Mr. Christian acted under an alias. They were reprinted in the December 15 edition of the *Evening Star* as follows:

University of Virginia
December 2, 1873
Dr. S.E. French
Dear Sir:
     The last mail brought your letter. Please send me at once two subjects of merchantable quality and securely barreled. I have had infinite trouble in consequence of a bloody liquid escaping from one of the barrels last winter. Send them by freight to Dr. J.S. Davis, University of Va., and notify me by mail that you have sent them.
Yours truly,
J.S. Davis
P.S. If the arrangement works well, I will get from you chiefly.

The preceding letter allows that the writer, Dr. Davis, has received bodies by shipment in the past, although presumably not from Mr. Christian or Dr. French. Previous transport must have provided inadequate packaging. The leakage of serosanguinous substance which he mentions surely proved difficult to explain to porters handling the barrels addressed to him. His instructions note that the bodies must be "of merchantable quality," an indication that he expects them to be as fresh as possible. Quality was important if the bodies were to be used for teaching purposes.

Ann Arbor, Michigan
December 4, 1873
Dr. S.E. French
303 East Capitol Street
Washington, D.C.
Dear Sir:
    Boxes have come, or rather barrels. Do not send barrels; they always get the heads knocked in, and excites suspicion if they do not, as the subjects shake about so. The best way to pack is in a tight box three feet by two, or near that dimension, the subject having the legs and thighs flexed and head resting on chest. Sawdust packed about prevent odor and the subject from shaking about in the box. Two can be put in a single box a little larger than the one I describe. You may keep on sending until I am done work at $25 each for good ones. We sell for forty to the students all injected, and I have to get my pay for keeping the room and all incidental expenses: The express averages about $7 a subject, so you see the price you mention could not be afforded. Your money will be sent promptly on the receipt of goods, and you may send me just as fast as you can between now and January 1st. In haste.
Yours truly,
G.E. Frothingham

The instructions contained in Frothingham's letter seem to show a familiarity with body shipment that George Christian apparently lacked. Perhaps Christian was new to the shipping business in December of 1873. Frothingham exhibits a well developed knowledge of dead body packaging in this letter so that it can be assumed that he did this sort of business on other occasions. He also seems to have a clear idea of price, for bodies, for "express" charges, and for incidentals. His willingness to do business on as large a scale as Christian can supply before January 1 indicates that he is supplying cadavers for the winter term at a medical or anatomy school, possibly the University of Michigan.

A well developed rail system probably enabled the shipment of corpses over long distances. There is some evidence that interstate business did occur and many of the later state laws contained provisions against shipment of cadavers across state lines. But the truth probably rests closer to home, i.e., the nearer the cemetery, the less chance of detection during transport of the body from grave to dissecting room.

Humphrey (p. 819) noted that black bodies were much more frequently snatched than white. In New York state in the late 1700s, rumors were that few blacks were left to rest in their graves. Blacks, like white almshouse residents, had very limited political voice or social standing. Objections to the grave robbers' activities, when they did arise, were often the result of extreme provocation. In obtaining cadavers for anatomic study, Dr. Richard Bayley's students from Columbia caused the following petition from free blacks and slaves to be made to New York City's council in 1788:

> ....[I]t hath lately been the constant practice of a number of the young gentlemen in this city who call themselves students of physick, to repair to the burying ground assigned for the use of your petitioners, under the cover of night, and in the most wanton sallies of excess, to dig up the bodies of the deceased friends and relatives of your petitioners, carry them away and without respect to age or sex, mangle their flesh out of a wanton curiosity and then expose it to Beasts and Birds. That your petitioners are well aware of the necessity of physicians and surgeons consulting dead subjects for the benefit of mankind, and far from presupposing it an injury to the deceased, in particular circumstances and when conducted with that decency and propriety which the solemnity of such an occasion requires your petitioners humbly pray your Honors to take their case into consideration, and adopt such measures as may seem meet to prevent similar abuses in the future [Heaton p. 1862].

Dr. Bayley denied "removing the bodies of any person or persons, interred in any churchyard or cemetery, belonging to any place of public worship, and ...[had] not offered any sum of money to procure any human body so interred, for the purposes of dissection." He further noted "that no person or persons under his tuition have had any agency or concern in digging up or removing any dead body interred in any of the churchyards or cemeteries, to his knowledge or belief" (Hartwell p. 221).

Savitt (p. 337–340) recognized the propensity of pre–Civil War Southern physicians to use the bodies of blacks rather than whites for anatomical study and dissection. Medical colleges used black janitors and porters to obtain cadavers of other blacks. The Medical College of Georgia even *purchased* a man to carry out these disagreeable chores. His name was Grandison Harris. The black population was aware of the grave robbing and cadaver business but was powerless to do anything about it. The most they could hope for if they wished to remain in their graves was to die during the summer when classes were not in session and bodies decomposed rapidly.

The Snatch of Henry Sutherland

The story of the snatch of Henry Sutherland, the son of a runaway slave, in Brookville, Pinecreek Township, Pennsylvania, in 1857 tells of a very smooth exhumation. The events that followed the resurrection caused the young doctors considerably more difficulty. Sutherland, age 30, died in October 1857. Doctor J.G. Simons organized a group of local physicians, and on the night of October 31, they set out to recover the body. The technique used was the same as that described by Christison and in two hours time the task was completed. The next day, one of the party divulged the nature of the previous night's activities and the body had to be removed from the intended dissection theater. On November 4, the body was moved to an icehouse where the dissection was to take place. The physicians, by this time fearful of discovery, skinned the body and removed fingers and toes to prevent identification and made plans to remove it from town. The key to the building was lost and the door had to be broken open. The wagon which was to transport the body arrived before the door was opened and continued on its way when the body could not be secured. The following day the body was discovered by the townspeople who opened Sutherland's grave to confirm their suspicion of the identity of the corpse. The body was reinterred on November 8, in a somewhat more mutilated condition than at his first burial (Montgomery p. 375–379).

The report of the incident in the *Brookville Jeffersonian*, Thursday, November 12, 1857, included an editorial comment on the practice of grave robbing and dissection.

> But when we reflect, that if persons can be permitted to enter the enclosure of the last resting place of the dead, and steal from its coffin the remains of a deceased darkey, carry it to an icehouse, skin it, tear out the bowels, cut off the toes and [fingures], and leave the mutilated remains in a place where it may chance to be discovered and be gazed upon by hundreds, and that we have no assurance but our bodies, or those of our friends may be treated in the same manner, cold and hardened must be the wretch who does not feel the flame of indignation raise in his breast at the perpetration of such an offense.
>
> If physicians desired the body, and had hired any person to dig it up and replace the dirt in the grave in the manner in which this was done, and had observed a degree of secrecy and care in the whole transaction, they might have obtained invaluable information and the world would be ignorant of their doings; but for their carelessness in this transaction, in leaving the body in an open house, uncovered, where any person was at liberty to step up to the door and peep in, they merit the censure of the whole community; *not for their seeking after knowledge, but for the barbarous and inhumane manner in which they conducted the affair,* and their carelessness in suffering their subject to be discovered and gazed at by hundreds who were attracted to it through curiosity.

Noteworthy in this commentary is the acknowledgment that physicians should attempt to improve their knowledge and skill, even through dissection of human bodies, but that these activities should be carried out in secret. The editors seem to be more outraged by the public discovery of the body than by the purpose for which it was acquired. Whether this attitude was generally held by the population is difficult to determine. The issue was not further addressed in the *Jeffersonian*.

Attempts at Prevention of Body Snatching

Citizens resorted to many ingenious methods to prevent the disinterment of their loved ones by body snatchers. Grave watchers, burial vaults, trip lines, carefully patterned graves, cemetery walls, locked gates, and other booby traps were fairly common. More typical of Britain than the United States was the use of impenetrable patented coffins and mortsafes. A few of these massive iron cages may still be seen in Greyfriars Churchyard in England. Mob violence sometimes resulted from blatant grave robbing activities but it did little to further the cause of prevention. The Resurrection riots of the United States are described in the order in which they occurred.

Families who had the means hired grave watchers. These individuals sat with the grave until such time as the body was sufficiently decomposed to be of no use for anatomic study. Churchyards sometimes had watchhouses where a fireplace and benches served to provide some small comfort to those who watched. Alcohol also aided in filling in time. Outsmarting the watchers was a game at which the determined resurrectionists excelled.

There are two examples, both from Britain, that illustrate the successful pursuit of a desired subject.

The first was that of a hydrocephalic child who was interred in a cemetery near the Firth of Forth. Grave watchers resisted all temptations and the test of patience between resurrectionists and watchers gradually subsided. The watchers continued to attend to their duty even when the situation relaxed.

One evening at dusk two well-dressed gentlemen, smoking their cigars, drove up in a dog-cart to the chief hostelry of the little burgh; they alighted, and requested that their horse might be taken care of for an hour. The 'whip-hand' gentleman told the ostler that he expected a livery servant to bring a parcel for him, which could be put in the box part of the conveyance, to which a key was attached. In a short time a man in smart livery came to the stable-yard, deposited a bag under the seat of the dog-cart, pocketed the key, and walked off—a canny silent man, or dull o'hearing.

When the watchers went to the cemetery as usual, they found the grave disturbed and the body missing. It was stolen in broad daylight in 30 minutes (Lonsdale: *The Life of Robert Knox* p. 66–68).

The second illustrative case is of the Irish giant, Charles Byrne (or O'Brien), who died in 1783. Mr. Byrne was an astonishing eight feet two inches tall. He was also given to drink, slightly retarded and probably tubercular. John Hunter, the famed English surgeon, wanted the giant's skeleton and made an attempt to buy it through an agent from Byrne before his death. Callous as it seems, this practice was not unheard of and often provided drinking money or perhaps pickling for future anatomical material. Byrne was also aware of Hunter's desire as he was watched closely by Howieson, the agent. In order to avoid being anatomized, Byrne left orders that following his death, his body was to be watched until such time as a lead coffin could be made and his remains sunk in the mouth of the Thames. No one is exactly sure how the snatch was effected but it is said that Hunter located the pub where the Irish watchers gathered and offered them a sum to allow the body to be removed. Rumor is that he eventually paid 500 pounds to secure the cadaver. Hunter was in such fear of discovery that he returned home immediately and boiled the flesh from the bones in his basement. If true, the brownish color of the bones of a giant displayed in the Hunter museum may be attributed to their hasty preparation. Speculation that Byrne may have been a victim of Cushing's syndrome was never proven (Packard p. 67; McAlister p. 257).

Grave watchers did occasionally accomplish their purpose. In Cincinnati, the grave of a young woman who had many admirers was closely guarded against snatchers. Some medical students who set about resurrecting her were greeted by gunshots from the belfry tower of the nearby church. Most of them escaped, but one unfortunate young man took a bullet through the eyelid and into the globe. Body snatching was a serious, sometimes fatal, sport (Baldwin p. 756).

Samuel Warren in the *Diary of a Late Physician* describes "my first and last exploit in the way of body-stealing." In a chapter entitled "Grave Doings" Dr. Warren presents the details of a case of a woman who was admitted to the hospital with symptoms that proved baffling to the physicians in attendance. Her family realized that she was seriously ill and in order to prevent her dissection by physicians removed her from the hospital to home. She subsequently died with her illness undiagnosed.

The doctors, who were immensely interested to find the cause of death, discovered when and where the girl was to be buried and determined to steal her body. They attempted to employ a professional body snatcher (whom they called a "grab"), but unfortunately found him to be drunk. They then secured the services of a porter from the hospital and a coach driver.

Arriving at the cemetery with moonlight fading, the doctors ordered the coach parked in a lane by the churchyard wall. With some fear that the girl's brothers might be watching the grave, coupled with inexperience at resurrectioning and a natural discomfort at visiting a graveyard at midnight, the four scaled the wall and entered the yard. A thunderstorm came up while they were attempting to locate the freshly dug grave during which all participants got thoroughly soaked. When they found the grave, they proceeded to open it digging two to a shift. To their immense discouragement, the grave was six feet deep and required much effort to open.

While they were engaged in digging, they were disturbed once by a donkey or mule that was grazing in the churchyard and came to investigate the noise.

In addition, their coachman, who was concerned by the length of time the project was taking, appeared at the site. His presence thoroughly frightened the four, who scattered to hide behind tombstones. The porter fell into a freshly opened, but unoccupied, grave from which he could not escape without help. When they finally discovered the identity of the visitor, all returned to the opened grave, removed the body, stripped it of grave clothes, sacked it up, and took it to the coach. Three remained to refill the grave.

But their troubles were not yet over. The coach was not where they had left it. The horses had moved off the street to graze and overturned the vehicle in a ditch. With a great deal of effort, the coach was righted and the party arrived back at town — broad daylight.

Warren reports that the subsequent dissection revealed that the girl died of "disease of the heart — but of too complicated a nature to be made intelligible to general readers" (Warren p. 94–109).

Sir Astley Cooper brands this account a fake in his general comments about the method of grave robbing. He states, "such a description of this proceeding has already been given to the public by one of the most popular and talented, but, in this case at least, fictitious authors of the day" (Cooper, volume 1, p. 350).

Dr. Warren's verification of the authenticity of the account in the *Diary* is included with his volume. "The Editor of these papers begs to inform all those who are so good as to transmit to him, 'Subjects for Passages' — to be 'worked up in his peculiar way' — that they have totally mistaken the character of this series of papers, in imagining them to be anything else than what they profess to be — the bona fide results of the individual's experience. Neither the Editor of these 'Passages,' nor their original writer, is any 'gatherer of other men's stuff" (Warren p. 109).

Burial vaults, such as the one erected by the Philadelphia Almshouse, fulfilled the same purpose. A burial vault is a building used as a depository for safekeeping of a body during the interval between death and interment.

Burial vaults usually had very thick walls and stout doors secured with several locks. An official was usually detailed to guard the vault, at least in the case of the Philadelphia Almshouse, and strict rules were adopted for the preservation of bodies in an unmutilated condition in cases where family or friends were known or could be found. "A messenger [was] always dispatched forthwith to inform the relatives or friends of the deceased in order that they may have the opportunity of removing the body; and it [was] always ... enjoined on the resident physicians and students never to make any examinations, unless with the express permission of the friends" (Lawrence p. 158).

Families who could not afford such luxuries attempted cheaper, but often just as effective, deterrents. Heavy planks or an iron slab placed across the roughbox made the exhumation difficult and, if placed lengthwise, all but impossible to access the head of the coffin.

To resurrect a body under these circumstances, the entire grave would have to be opened to remove the planks, a task which body snatchers were unwilling to perform. Some assert that snatchers resolved this problem by removing the body either through the end or side of the coffin with hooks. Even if this was true, none of these hooks has ever been found.

Another ploy was to fill the grave with stones. Stones were heavier and noisier than loose earth and thus, the chances of discovery of a clandestine raid were increased. Graves might also be marked with a particular pattern of sticks, stones, and or flowers. A disturbance detected in the pattern was evidence that a snatch had occurred. Resurrectionists, however, were experts in returning all items to the proper place since careful attention to details ensured the success of their mission. Cooper (p. 378) mentions that a coffin was sometimes filled with quicklime, or perhaps buried so deep that the water table covered it.

Since body snatchers usually scaled churchyard walls for access to burial grounds rather than enter through the main gate, glass and other sharp objects were sometimes implanted along the top of the wall. Walls might also be erected six to eight feet above the usual height, with the top few layers of brick or stone left loose. Trip lines attached to guns or spring guns were also occasionally used. Resurrectionists avoided these by reconnoitering the yard during the day, locating the lines and guns, and dismantling them before setting about the task of digging.

Christison (p. 180) describes massive iron cages, called mortsafes, to prevent resurrectionists from disturbing graves. A mortsafe was plalced over one or more graves or a vault, and secured in a concrete foundation. The door or gate was fitted with a lock. Another style of mortsafe consisted of massive stone slabs fitted with iron latticework underneath and buried over the top of the coffin. Some were shaped like a water trough and placed upside down over the coffin (Mitchell p. 426–427). The mortsafe was an option open to rich families who owned the land in which their dead were interred. Poorer families who did not own cemetery lots in perpetuity could not afford such luxury.

Use of iron coffins experienced brief popularity in the early 1800s. The best known of these was Edward Lillie Bridgman's Patented Iron (Cole p. 44), which was constructed entirely of wrought iron and had no exterior hinges, screws, or other moving parts. The cost approximated that of a wood coffin.

The only problem was that some sextons refused burial in their churchyards when an iron coffin was used. Exclusive use of the nearly imperishable iron boxes would have filled the burial grounds to capacity in a few short years. Bridgman of Goswell Street Road was apparently not the only maker of patented coffins. The poem "The Surgeon's Warning" includes a reference to a maker in St. Martin's Lane. While the iron coffin was billed as an insuperable obstacle to grave robbers, it fell short of the claim. They could be opened by breaking the lid with a sledgehammer, an effective but noisy process. Neither iron coffins nor mortsafes ever achieved much popularity in this country.

Resurrection Riots

Charles Darwin, while in medical training in Edinburgh, witnessed a mob attacking two resurrectionists as he walked with a botanist friend. He described the incident in his autobiography.

> I once saw in his company in the streets of Cambridge almost as horrid a scene as could have been witnessed during the French Revolution. Two body-snatchers had been arrested, and whilst being taken to prison had been torn from the constable by a crowd of the roughest men who dragged them by their legs along the muddy and stony road. They were covered from head to foot with mud, and their faces were bleeding, either from having been kicked or from the stones; they looked like corpses, but the crowd was so dense that I got only a few momentary glimpses of the wretched creatures. Never in my life have I seen such wrath painted on a man's face as was shown by Henslow [the botanist with whom Darwin walked] at this horrid scene. He tried repeatedly to penetrate the mob; but it was simply impossible. He then rushed away to the mayor, telling me not to follow him, but to get more policemen. I forget the issue, except that the two men were got into the prison without being killed (Robinson p. 337).

Americans are not without similar occurrences. The earliest incident was in Philadelphia. William Shippen's activities relative to the establishment of anatomy courses in 1765 aroused Philadelphians to such a fever that Shippen found his life in danger. His experience is recorded in the chapter on Dissection for Education. His defense appeared as a disclaimer notice in the newspaper in which he maintained that he dissected only criminals or occasionally one from Potter's Field.

In New York in April 1788 a riot occurred as a result of the activities of a rambunctious medical student who waved a dismembered limb out of one of the upper story windows of New York Hospital. A number of children playing in the yard below witnessed this immature display and borrowed a ladder to get a better view.

When they peeked in the third story window, they beheld human cadavers, both black and white, in various stages of dissection and dismemberment. An angry mob collected and for several days threatened physicians and medical students throughout the city. Eventually it was dispersed by New York militiamen. A more detailed account appears in *The Coming of the Anatomy Laws.*

Dr. Charles F. Wiesenthal, sometimes called the father of the medical profession in Baltimore, came to the United States from Prussia in 1755. He started an anatomy school behind his home on Gay Street and taught students there until his death.

In 1788, a mob invaded his dissecting rooms and demanded the body of a murderer named Cassiday on which they were working. Patrick Cassiday, along with John Webb, was executed for the murder of Capt. John De Corse, the master of a ship on which they were passengers in May of 1788 (Cordell p. 15). The students complied and released the body (Krumbhaar: Early history of anatomy, p. 284).

In 1807 in Baltimore another resurrection riot occurred for a similar reason. This incident was also the result of some curious boys peeking into a dissection room. Angry citizens destroyed the Anatomy Hall of Dr. John Beale Davidge located at the Medical Department of the University of Maryland. Dr. Davidge was a private teacher of anatomy and the buildings that were destroyed were erected on the grounds at his own expense (Hartwell p. 224; Cordell p. 55). As a result of the mob's actions, the school remained deserted for the next seven years. It was not until some 25 years later that the reinitiated school again required an anatomy laboratory in the medical curriculum.

In 1811, Zanesville, Ohio, local citizens found a desecrated grave in the middle of the winter. The tracks of the wheelbarrow used in the transport of the body led searchers to a hotel where some medical students resided. The body was discovered in the basement behind a woodpile. The hotel appears to have been the only victim. It was reduced to rubble.

Yale Medical College was the scene of a riot in January 1824. On a cold Saturday night or Sunday morning, a corpse was resurrected from the West

Haven burial yard. The victim, if she could be called so, was a young woman by the name of Bathsheba Smith, the daughter of Laban Smith, a respected local farmer. Poor grave robbing technique led to the discovery. The careless perpetrators failed to shade the lantern adequately during their labors. The outraged townspeople sought out a General Kimberly and caused him to issue a search warrant for the buildings and grounds of Yale Medical School. The warrant was duly served by the constable, Erastus Osborn, to Dr. Jonathan Knight.

All three, General Kimberly, Constable Osborn, and Dr. Knight, set out early Monday morning to execute the search. The record has been preserved in the letters of Constable Osborn to his father, Shadrack Osborn. Shadrack was the postmaster of a nearby town. After covering the college from top to bottom, the searchers discovered the body in a cellar under some large flagstones in a crypt some three feet by two feet.

Bathsheba was taken up from her temporary quarters, washed, clothed and returned to West Haven. So great was the outcry of the people, that the medical students barricaded themselves in at the college. Discretion being the better part of valor, the constable recorded that he "intended to keep at home and let the ferment have vent or subside." And have vent it did. During the week that followed there was rioting nearly every night. Several arrests were made.

Three students were apparently involved in the snatch. Two escaped, but the third, Ephraim Colborn, was arrested. The situation was so volatile that young Colborn barely escaped tarring and feathering.

In January, Ephraim Colborn was tried for robbing a grave of a body to be used for dissection. He pleaded not guilty. Evidence was entirely circumstantial; no one saw him commit the act. Nevertheless, he was convicted and sentenced to nine months in jail and assessed a $300.00 fine. Just exactly what Colborn was convicted of is difficult to determine since Connecticut did not have any statutes at that time to cover grave robbing. It appears that in the face of threatened violence, justice miscarried (Hamlin).

Connecticut passed a dissection law in 1824, after the conviction of Colborn, but only as a posthumous punishment for capital crimes.

Worthington Medical College in Ohio, the first chartered sectarian medical college in the United States, was the scene of a riot in 1839. Citizens gathered to register their displeasure at the grave robberies in the area and rumored dissections which were attributed to the school. The school was destroyed but managed to grant a few degrees in February 1840 just before the Ohio legislature rescinded its charter in March of that year. Worthington resurfaced two years later in 1842 under the name of the Reformed Medical College of Cincinnati, but a charter was not granted. It was not until 1845 that the school again began legitimate operation, with a charter,

under the name of Eclectic Medical Institute (Waite: Second medical school
p. 1336).

In 1844, a resurrection riot occurred in St. Louis. McDowell Medical
College (or the Missouri Medical College) was destroyed by local citizens.
The following year the college became a part of the University of Missouri
(Norwood p. 399).

As late as 1847, Willoughby Medical College (Ohio) was forced by a
mob to relocate. It moved to Columbus, where it became the Ohio State
University Medical School (Lassek p. 235).

Any deterrent effect that newspaper editorials and letters, irate
citizens, or mob violence might have had on grave robbing was temporary
at best. It was not until the enactment of anatomy laws that the practice
of body snatching abated to the level where the interred remained in the
ground.

Political Fallout from a Grave Robbing

Governor Arthur Fenner accused Judge John Dorrance (both of Rhode
Island) of having sold in February 1799 the body of a stranger who committed suicide by hanging. The body was purportedly offered to a local physician, Dr. Pardon Bowen, who then allegedly paid Judge Dorrance one
beaver hat for the privilege of possession. Governor Fenner used the charge
to engineer the political defeat of the Judge's campaign for a seat in the
General Assembly in 1801. In response, Judge Dorrance sued Governor
Fenner for slander.

Amid a bevy of newspaper attacks and General Assembly resolutions,
trials commenced in December 1801. Charges were cross-actions for
slander. Not one shred of evidence was produced to support Governor Fenner's contention of wrongdoing by the Judge. The body was indeed stolen
and dissected, but not with Judge Dorrance's knowledge or approval. Nor
was he paid a beaver hat for the corpse.

The first trial ended in a verdict of costs to be paid to the governor,
but the jury's decision was not unanimous. Ignoring that no accord could
be reached, the verdict was recorded and the jury was dismissed. the second trial began in January 1802 with the same jury reinstated less the dis-
senting juror. However, a decision for a change of location for teh second trial resulted in selection of a new jury. Selection was so biased that
Judge Dorrance gave up and the court awarded the governor $10,000 plus
costs.

In spite of overwhelming evidence to the contrary, Dorrance lost both
cases, paid court costs for both trials and was cheated out of a seat in the
General Assembly of Rhode Island. Although Judge Dorrance was of good

character and by all accounts well-liked, it appears that the mere charge of body snatching was sufficient to cost him the election. Perhaps that is a further indication of the public sentiment against such activities.

The body was dissected over a period of several days during the month of February 1799 by a group of six or eight physicians and medical students.

Valentine Mott, M.D.

Dr. Valentine Mott (1785–1865), a noted American surgeon and outstanding surgical teacher, was convinced of the value of the study of anatomy and dissection in medical education. His own medical experience in Europe brought him into contact with such great anatomists and surgeons as Abernethy, Bell, Cooper, and Monro. Gross describes Mott as a fearless operator because he was unmoved by the sight of blood and because he was well versed in topographical and relative anatomy. He had a large collection of morbid specimens which were destroyed in a fire at the medical department of the University of the City of New York in 1866. Mott was distraught over the loss of such valued teaching aids (Gross p. 308–309).

Dr. Mott was also a body snatcher par excellence. Once, by his own admission, he drove at night to a graveyard where, dressed as a common laborer, he received 11 cadavers that his comrades had unearthed. These he drove to the medical college while perched on top of his cargo (Kelly and Burrage p. 881). Mott's visits to potter's fields for dissecting material were not unique. It is said that the first six presidents of the New York Academy of Medicine (1847, John Stearns, M.D.; 1848, John Wakefield Francis, M.D.; 1849, Valentine Mott, M.D.; 1850, Isaac Wood, M.D.; 1851, Alexander H. Stevens, M.D.; 1852, Thomas Cock, M.D.) acknowledged that they had participated in body snatching during either their student or early medical practice days.

Not all Dr. Mott's attempts at body snatching went so smoothly. He and a colleague, accompanied by a porter, set out on a cold evening to recover a body. Mott's colleague deserted the party, complaining that he was ill, and returned home. After the grave was opened the porter refused to touch the body. Dr. Mott was forced to retrieve the corpse from the grave alone and drag it to the coach unassisted (Heaton p. 1863).

Joseph N. McDowell, M.D., Grandiloquent Yet Insecure

Dr. Joseph McDowell, a pretentious character on the surface but rather timid underneath, was a brilliant and learned anatomy teacher.

Students loved him because he made "the dry bones talk." One night, Dr. McDowell set out to rob a grave, for even though he was afraid, he felt that visiting a cemetery at night was a mark of courage. On his return, a severe thunderstorm overtook him. McDowell was extremely afraid of thunderstorms, and he became more disconcerted as the storm worsened. After a particularly loud thunderclap, the doctor heard the sound of a shot and, turning around, looked upon the corpse. It was sitting up with a pistol in its shriveled hand. He became so frightened that he deserted the wagon to make his escape. As he related his tale to his class the next day, the students cheered him, which caused him to elaborate and exaggerate his hair-raising experience. Little did he realize that he was the victim of a hoax perpetrated by his students (Flexner p. 222).

In another of Dr. McDowell's exploits, he ventured into a graveyard to resurrect the body of a girl who died of an unusual disease. He barely had time to make his escape to the college when the girl's friends and relatives discovered her missing body and set out in vigilante style to recover it. Finding himself in the building besieged by the mob, McDowell threw the cadaver over his shoulder and headed for the attic. Once the body was secreted there, he realized that he was trapped in a building with the goods. He returned to the dissecting room whereupon his lamp went out. There, in the dark, the ghost of his dear, departed mother came to his rescue and bade him stretch out on the dissecting table from which he had just removed the cadaver. This he did, frantically pulling a sheet over his head just as the angry crowd swarmed into the room. They peeked under the sheet and remarked upon the freshness of this corpse. McDowell wrote, "I thought I would jump up and frighten them, but I heard a voice, soft and low, close to my ear, say 'Be still, be still.'" Finally the mob departed and McDowell, through yet another scrape, arose and subsequently boasted to anyone who would listen of his daring adventure (Flexner p. 223–224).

Philip Syng Physick, M.D., The Squeamish Anatomist

Philip Syng Physick was born in 1768 and died December 15, 1837. He studied medicine in England and was a student of John Hunter. He was a conservative and an honest surgeon, preferring to save a limb rather than amputate. One of the last operations he performed before his death was a lithotomy on Chief Justice John Marshall in which he removed nearly one thousand calculi; the patient made an excellent recovery. Samuel David Gross wrote, "Physick was essentially an empiric, practising altogether in the light of experience. He had no theories of his own and was intolerant in his teachings and his practice of the theories of others. . . . He troubled himself little respecting the pathology or intimate nature of disease. In short, he was what is generally known as a routine practitioner" (Gross p. 244).

Benjamin Rush, M.D., author of the monumental treatise on *Diseases of the Mind* and famous early American physician, died in April 1813. A contemporary of Philip Syng Physick, M.D., one of the fine surgeons of Philadelphia, Rush was not known to be a particular friend to Dr. Physick. The following account appears in the Centennial Volume of the *Transactions of the College of Physicians*, 1887, and was related by John Ashhurst, Jr.

Late in the evening of the day Rush was buried, Physick was aroused from his sitting room in the upstairs of his house and called to his door by loud ringing of the doorbell. His caller was a large black man who demanded, "Do you want Dr. Rush?"

Completely taken aback, Physick responded, "What do you mean? Dr. Rush is dead." The caller retorted that he knew that and would supply his body to the college by nine o'clock the next morning for $20. Physick, who possessed a natural distaste for practical anatomy, refused the offer. He was both shocked and terrified by the event.

Although Physick died almost a quarter of a century later, he made careful preparations so that his mortal remains would not find their way to the dissecting room. He refused a post mortem and provided that only two female attendants from his house were to receive his body after death. Further he was to be left in his house, in his bed, in a heated bedroom, and wrapped in flannel blankets. After such time as his body was sufficiently decayed, he was to be placed in a coffin, and that coffin to be placed in a sealed lead coffin. These wishes were followed and there can be little doubt that Dr. Physick rests undisturbed in his grave (Haviland p. 774–775).

Dr. Thomas Sewall, Amateur Body Snatcher

On a cold, snowy night in January 1818, Ipswich, Massachusetts, was the scene of a grave robbery. Lights were seen in the cemetery but because of the snowfall all tracks were obliterated. It was suspected that resurrectionists were at work to recover the body of Sally Andrews, who had died on Christmas Day 1817. When the snow melted, a hair ornament identified as belonging to the young woman was found. An investigation ensued and it was soon discovered that not just one, but eight graves were empty. These belonged to three men, two women, two boys and a servant. A reward of $500 was offered for information leading to the detection of the perpetrator. As a reminder, the eight coffins were left open to public view for three months.

Eventually, parts of three bodies were discovered in the possession of Dr. Thomas Sewall. He was using them to teach operative surgery to a group of young medical students. Dr. Sewall was indicted on three counts, one for each body. On the plea of his attorney, Daniel Webster, one count was tabled because it was inaccurately drawn. He was tried in November 1819 on the remaining two counts and convicted of possession of the corpses. The charge stated that "Thomas Sewall did knowingly and wilfully receive, conceal, and dispose of the human body and remains thereof of one Sally Andrews" and William Burnham. He was fined $800 and court costs, a stupendous fine for 1819. The conviction was not for grave robbing, but the possession of bodies.

Dr. Sewall's reputation as well as his medical practice in Ipswich were destroyed. Daniel Webster, then serving as a congressman, invited Sewall to Washington, D.C. There he began a highly successful medical career and subsequently founded the antecedent of the George Washington University School of Medicine in 1825 (Waite [1939] p. 225; Lassek p. 189–190).

"Yea, Lord, I'm Coming—"

Four resurrectionists—two medical students, an elderly black man, and a boy—set out one July to recover the body of a young man recently deceased of a rare disease. They scaled the fence enclosing the burial ground and located the grave. The elderly man, who carried the spades, and the boy, who brought the ropes, began the operation of recovering the body. The two students watched. When the coffin was uncovered and the ropes secured so that the resurrection could be accomplished, the students pitched in. Just at the moment the coffin was to be lifted, one of the students remarked in a serious voice, "Arise, and come to judgment!" Much to their surprise, there arose a white-clad figure from behind a neighboring tombstone who responded with equal seriousness, "Yea, Lord, I'm coming." The resurrectionists' disorderly departure from the cemetery was accomplished with all due haste to the village where they related their tale, no doubt through chattering teeth.

On the following day, the townspeople ventured to the cemetery but found no evidence of grave robbery or disturbance.

The story apparently circulated, and some time later a stranger avowed that he had had exactly the same experience. It appears that he was trying to find his way home after an evening of carousing and lost his sense of direction. He decided to take a short nap and was awakened by the rather loud proclamation of the medical student. It was this gentleman who covered up the grave and departed the burial ground with the tools of the would-be resurrectionists (Philadelphia *Public Ledger* June 8, 1839).

The Wild West

Body snatching stories from the old west are not so plentiful as those from east of the Mississippi. Several reasons for this may be inferred. Medical schools were more plentiful and founded earlier in the east, before the enactment of anatomy laws. Doctors who traveled west were already educated, even if in the eclectic and homoeopathic methods rather than the regular, orthodox medical traditions. Little time was afforded the scientific pursuits; life was hard and travel long to cover a small practice. Indians, too, were numerous, and much as in early New England, they probably fell prey to the inquiring surgeon's knife. Richard Dunlop's *Doctors of the American Frontier* contains an account of just such a scientific pursuit.

The scene was San Antonio, Texas. It was March of 1840 and an indian war was going on right outside of town. Some of the ladies had gathered on a porch for tea and social discourse to savor the settlers' victory. The local doctor, whose name was Weideman, rode up to the porch and, excusing himself as any gentleman would, proceeded to place two severed Indian heads on the window sill for display. Next he unloaded the bodies from his horse, commenting that he was extremely lucky to have obtained two such excellent specimens. The conversation at the tea party was, as one might imagine, somewhat inhibited. The ladies dispersed and the doctor went in search of a wagon in which to transport his prizes home.

That night, Dr. Weideman boiled the cadavers in a large vat to loosen the flesh so that he could secure the skeletons. The bones were laid out to dry and the Indian stew dumped into the Acequia river. It was this final outrage that brought about his arrest and trial. The river was the only source of water for the town, which was *downstream* from the doctor's residence. The thought that they had washed, eaten, and laundered in Indian broth was too much for the locals. Many were said to have been sick. Never mind that the vat was dumped early in the night and had by dawn washed far beyond San Antonio. No one believed that story.

The judge meted out a stiff fine and verbal thrashing to the enterprising doctor. The townspeople begged him to stick to curing the sick and letting this science business alone. He, in turn, agreed not to dump such disgusting contents into the Acequia in the future.

Owen Brown

John Brown's raid on Harper's Ferry, West Virginia, in 1859 for the purpose of acquiring the arms to engineer an invasion of the South and of encouraging a slave rebellion fired the imagination of the country. Brown and his 18 followers succeeded in capturing the federal arsenal there on October 16, 1859, but they failed to make a clean escape. Brown's son, Owen, did not participate in the capture of the fort but attempted instead to seize Hall's Rifle Works by the Shenandoah River. Nearly all the men who participated in this excursion were killed or escaped into the mountains. Robert E. Lee, then a colonel, recaptured the fort on October 18 and turned Brown and his remaining followers over for trial. The students at Winchester Medical College in Virginia decided on a field trip to Harper's Ferry to see some of the action for themselves. Upon disembarkation from the train, they discovered a freshly deceased body close to the bank of the Shenandoah River. The possibilities for its use immediately occurred to the students and the body was crated up and shipped back to the college. Later examination of the clothes and papers revealed that the cadaver was none other than Owen Brown, son of John Brown. Owen's death wound appeared to be a shot directly into the umbilicus. Several other anatomical contributions from the Harper's Ferry raid made their way to the college via disinterment from the cemetery.

In March 1862, General Nathaniel P. Banks of the Union Army liberated the body of Owen Brown and returned it North for burial. The college buildings were burned, possibly in retaliation, but it made little difference since the college had ceased in April 1861. The buildings were being used as a military hospital (Packard p. 786–787; Blanton p. 71).

The James Gang's Contribution to Medical Education

In September 1876, the James-Younger gang attempted to rob the Northfield Bank in Northfield, Minnesota. Two citizens and two robbers were shot to death during the encounter. While the townspeople formed a posse and gave chase, a medical student from the University of Minnesota recognized the value of the bodies of the robbers as dissecting material. These two were disinterred, placed in kegs labeled "Fresh Paint," and shipped to Ann Arbor to the medical school. Relatives of one of the resurrected robbers reclaimed his body but no one claimed the second. The body subsequently served its scientific purpose and the skeleton accompanied the young physician, Henry Wheeler, to his practice in Grand Forks, North Dakota. Some 50 years later, fire destroyed Wheeler's office and with it, the skeleton (Holtz).

An Overzealous Policeman

It was the practice of students to remove bodies from the cemetery of the Columbus State Hospital in Ohio. One evening in 1878 some students from Columbus Medical College were engaged in the removal of the body of a recently deceased girl to the basement of the college when they were accosted by a policeman. Since the students' maneuvers had been overlooked by the police in the past, they freely revealed the nature of their business. Much to their chagrin, they found themselves in a bit of a pinch when the policeman arrested them.

Sometime during the night the body was placed in a shabby coffin and transported back to a cemetery, a sort of potter's field at the edge of town. The coffin was placed in a little shed. A physician from Columbus Hospital, Dr. C.P. Gailey, was called to identify the body. When the shed was opened and the coffin lid pried up, an enormous explosion of flies emerged. The physician was, however, able to positively affirm that the corpse was that of the girl stolen from Columbus and she was returned to be reburied. The policeman was relieved of his duties (Baldwin p. 756).

Samuel David Gross, M.D., Would-Be Body Snatcher

In 1883, Samuel D. Gross, M.D., was a practicing surgeon in Easton, Pennsylvania. It came to his attention that a drunken soldier had committed suicide by hanging himself. Gross determined to have the body for anatomical study. Calling upon a student at the University of Pennsylvania named Green, he expressed his desire. Late in the evening of the day of burial, Gross and two students set out with digging equipment and a wheelbarrow to a resurrection party. The grave was located with no difficulty and the work of removing the soil begun. The shovels made so much noise, however, that Gross elected to refill the grave and leave without disturbing the body. Several days later the brother of the deceased accosted Green and accused him of stealing the body. "Doctor," he said, "I believe you got my brother's body." Green neither admitted nor denied the charge and replied, "You can believe what you please" (Lassek p. 222).

A Midwinter Chase

In January 1885, the Minnesota College Hospital was experiencing a shortage of dissecting material. Two students, Paul Shillock and Thomas Salueva set out to collect a body purportedly available and already boxed at a local brickyard in Chaska, Minnesota. They arrived, found the box, transferred it to their wagon, and set out for Minneapolis. The temperature approached 35 below and the drive to their destination took four hours. They discovered to their dismay that they were being pursued by the local sheriff and a posse. Fearful of a lynching on the spot, Salueva abandoned the wagon and took to the woods. Shillock followed shortly thereafter. Both students wandered about in the woods for several hours, finally reuniting and trekking back to the College Hospital. Salueva was dressed less warmly, and thus suffered the effects of the cold more than his co-conspirator. He lost at least his toes and possibly his feet from severe frostbite. Both students endured the further ignominy of conviction for grave robbing (Smith p. 333–337).

Bodies Lost — and Found!

On October 13, 1846, the Philadelphia *Public Ledger* reported that a body had been found in the alley behind Franklin Medical College. It was sacked up, but the sack was open with the feet sticking out, and the gate partly ajar. Local citizens discovered the grisly sight about six o'clock in the morning. Franklin Medical College was new (the first graduating class was 1847) and the newspaper speculated that the ploy with the cadaver was an attempt to poison the public mind against the new medical school.

The coroner removed the body, having determined that it was deceased nine or ten days and in an extremely emaciated condition. Opinion was that the corpse was from either the almshouse or the county prison. It was reinterred. The public excitement gradually subsided.

A report from the *Public Ledger* in 1841 recounts the discovery of a human head in a culvert near Filbert and Tenth Streets. The coroner took charge of the find. The newspaper commented that it was probably not a case of murder since there was a medical college in the neighborhood.

Public concern in these two circumstances, both reported in the local daily paper, seems to have been mild when compared to the gravity of the discoveries. Bodies and body parts lying about streets must surely have been serious matters but it does not appear that positive identification of either of the deceased was made, although the report on the head was that it belonged to a black female.

Sir Astley Cooper, too, had bodies that arrived at inopportune moments and in the wrong places. Because of a disagreement between hospital porters and resurrection gangs in 1801, the body snatchers could not deliver their stock-in-trade to the dissecting rooms. In order that St. Thomas' Hospital would continue to have a sufficient supply of subjects to conduct anatomy classes, Sir Astley permitted the resurrectionists to deposit bodies in the courtyard of his home at St. Mary Axe. From there a man named Butler collected the subjects and transported them by coach to the hospital.

One night Butler collected three hampers that were deposited in the yard by a resurrectionist named Harnett. He ordered the hired coachman to drive him to the hospital, but instead the driver stopped at a local inn. The driver called to anyone who was listening that he was transporting a suspicious cargo. With that, Butler slipped out of the coach and returned to St. Mary Axe where he reported to Sir Astley's servant, Charles, what had happened. Several hours later, the coachman and a local watchman arrived at St. Mary Axe with a story about the discovery of three bodies in the hampers. Charles expressed surprise and disavowed any knowledge, his own or Sir Astley's, of the freight. The watchman insisted, however, on seeing Sir Astley and was shown to his bedroom. He learned little more from the great surgeon. Cooper would accept no responsibility for what was deposited in his yard or what might have been removed from it. The watchman, having received no satisfactory explanation, expressed his intention to see the Mayor the next morning. In this mission, he was preceded by none other than Sir Astley himself, who arrived while the mayor was eating breakfast. He presented the "facts" of the case and prevailed upon the mayor to assure that he would not be further molested about the matter. Such promise was secured (Cooper p. 341-343).

Another Business: The Market in Teeth

When the police accompanied Mrs. Bishop (see Bishop, May and Williams in Murder!) to the residence at No. 3 Nova Scotia Gardens, they took the opportunity to look around. The constable found two crowbars, a file, and a bradawl, an awl with a chisel edge for making holes for brads or screws. He remarked to Mrs. Bishop that this last tool was used for punching out teeth, which she denied. She said her husband used the instrument in shoe repair.

Teeth were nearly as valuable a commodity as the bodies themselves, and the resurrectionists were not averse to a little trade with the dentists on the side. Only the well-to-do could afford dentures; the molars were frequently made of ivory but the front teeth were human (Smout p. 80). Real teeth were prized for their durability and color. It is said that at least one body snatcher who gained access to a vault carried away not one body, but enough teeth to net 60 pounds for his night's work. Not all teeth were secured from subjects recovered from the grave.

Bransby Blake Cooper, nephew of Sir Astley Cooper, served as an assistant surgeon in the Royal Artillery during the Peninsular War. During his tour of duty in Spain in 1814, he was visited by Tom Butler, a body snatcher, with whom his uncle was acquainted. Butler was described by Bransby as a "short, stout, goodtempered man, with laughing eyes and a Sancho Panza sort of expression. He was much addicted to gin. When drunk, he was a great boaster, and inclined to be violent; but was easily cooled down by good-humored treatment" (Cooper p. 411). He began his career as a porter at St. Thomas and subsequently moved into his father's trade as an articulator of skeletons. It was later that he began to deal in teeth. Butler carried with him a letter of introduction from Sir Astley. This visit, Butler informed Bransby, was solely for the purpose of collecting the teeth from soldiers slain on the battlefield. His profit from the excursion was reported to be about 300 pounds (p. 402). When he returned to London, Butler set up a moderately successful practice in dentistry.

There is no indication in the literature that American body snatchers engaged in similar practices.

AMERICAN PROFESSIONALS

English literature abounds with tales of "professional" resurrectionists. A few professional American body snatchers existed, but they have remained relative unknowns. One such character is William Cunningham, a.k.a. Old Cunny, The Ghoul, and Old Dead Man, of Cincinnati, Ohio. "Old Cunny," a large, hard-drinking Irishman of unsavory reputation, was a wagon driver by day and a resurrectionist by night. His nighttime business supplied the medical schools in the area with enough cadavers (for which he charged $30 each) for the study of anatomy. Cunningham used some ingenious methods to transport cadavers. Once having obtained a body he would dress the corpse in old clothes and sit it in the wagon beside him. If anyone came within hearing distance, he would speak to the corpse as if it were alive, admonishing his companion for drunkenness by saying, "Sit up! This is the last time I am going to take you home when you get drunk. The idea of a man with a family disgracing himself this way!" Since Cunningham supplied customers outside the immediate Cincinnati area, he occasionally shipped bodies by mail. One such box was discovered bearing the label "Glass with care, C.O.D." and addressed to a Dr. Hayden in Leavenworth, Kansas.

William Cunningham was a fearless man. On one body snatching venture, he and his two companions stopped in a local tavern for a few drinks. Their manner alerted some of the locals who followed them when they departed. They were observed in the cemetery resurrecting a body and the posse moved in firing several shots. The two assistants fled immediately, but Old Cunny held his ground and refused to raise his hands. One of the men pointed a gun at him and fired, but it failed to discharge. With that, Cunny surrendered and the party left the cemetery. Along the way, they passed a tavern where the prisoner offered to buy some refreshment for his captors. The offer was accepted and after several rounds, Cunny was released with the admonition that he return directly to Cincinnati. Instead, he made his way back to the cemetery with every intention of completing the work begun. His assistants had already unearthed two cadavers and with these, the party did return to Cincinnati.

Cunningham, like many of his English resurrectionist counterparts, was also vindictive. He is said to have been the victim of a joke that he repaid by supplying the unsuspecting medical students with the body of a small pox victim. Cunningham was caught with two cadavers on August 31, 1871, and indicted for his activities. He died in October of that same year, but before his death sold his own body to the Medical College of Ohio for $5. His skeleton graces the museum (Edwards).

Another professional who operated in Ohio was Dr. Charles O. Morton, an alias of Dr. Henri Le Caron. Le Caron, a graduate of the Detroit Medical College, began his grave robbing exploits to support his education while still a medical student. Here he began the business of selling bodies to the University of Michigan (Kaufman p. 31–32). "Dr. Morton" had several other aliases, among them Gabriel and Dr. Christian. Together with Henry Morton, a brother, and Thomas Beverly (a.k.a. Johnson), he conducted a regular business in body snatching. Under contract to a firm called A.H. Jones and Company, they supplied bodies to this Ann Arbor, Michigan, concern. When they were arrested in Toledo, Ohio, in 1878, they were engaged in filling an order for 70 bodies, 60 of which had already been shipped. Morton escaped before he could be brought to trial. He may have been involved in the resurrection of Augustus Devin, who was buried next to John Scott Harrison in North Bend, Ohio (Edwards, pamphlet p. 16, 21).

L.S. Eaton (a.k.a. Evans), Cap Hilliard and Dr. Irwin Heyl were arrested in 1879 for illegally disinterring bodies in the Zanesville, Ohio, area. Eaton was a professional body snatcher who supplied local as well as distant medical schools with cadavers. Columbus was their usual base of operations (Edwards, pamphlet).

Shortly after the Civil War, Washington, D.C., attracted a large number of resurrectionists. The war had shown battlefield surgeons the value of knowledge of anatomy and the medical profession set out to correct the deficiencies of medical education. A professional resurrectionist named Janssen sought to fill the demand for cadavers by raiding some of the better class cemeteries in the Washington area, an act for which he was arrested quite often. His activities were not confined to the immediate area and he was known to have plied his trade as far away as Baltimore.

Like his European counterparts, Janssen was totally unscrupulous, selling bodies to one medical school, stealing them back, and reselling them to another. Charlie Shaw was executed on January 19, 1883, for the murder of his sister. Charlie was barely in his grave before Janssen had him up and sold to a medical college. Janssen felt, however, that he had not received sufficient recompense for his efforts and swore revenge. On the night of January 22, he engaged a hack and driver, Johnny Mack, and went to the college where the body was recovered. The rest of the night was spent in a vain attempt to unload the body on another medical school. With dawn upon them and no resolution to the problem, Janssen simply left his drunken partner with the "goods." With the legs of the corpse hanging out of the cab window, Mack drove the wagon to the police station. But Johnny Mack was not Janssen's undoing. He was arrested at a tavern where he was overheard bragging about his exploits. For this foray, he spent a year in jail (Eliot p. 251–252). In final exasperation, the medical schools took up a collection to bribe this ruffian to depart. The last trace of him was in 1884 (Lassek p. 231).

George Christian, a government clerk employed in the Surgeon General's Office in Washington, D.C., ran a little grave robbing and shipping business on the side. He and four others (Percy Brown, Maude Brown, Margaret Harrison, and "Workhouse" Kate) maintained a small shack which served as a holding room for shrouds, clothing, and other items secured from graveyards. The bodies were injected and packed in whiskey barrels, rolled to the Army Medical Museum, and shipped from there. Christian personally oversaw the shipment at the museum, for each body brought between $40 and $100 depending upon the demand.

Percy Brown and his sister (or wife?) Maude Pratt (Brown) developed their own modus operandi. Maude, appropriately dressed and veiled, appeared as the chief mourner at funerals, shedding copious tears and accompanying the coffin to the cemetery. When the closing came, she would beg a few flowers from the coffin of the deceased, her dear friend. These she surreptitiously dropped close to the grave, thus marking it for later resurrection.

Christian was described as an athletic man of medium build with black hair and beard. He was well dressed owing to his supply of clothing from corpses. Like so many others of his ilk, he was a heavy drinker which eventually caused his ruination. He and his party were stopped on a Washington street in December 1873. They had been to Holmead's cemetery resurrectioning and were rather intoxicated. They were arrested by Officer McGlue and charged with carrying concealed weapons, drunk and disorderly conduct, and suspicious conduct. The body of Thomas Fletcher was discovered in a sack along with chemicals for injection and a syringe. A search of the prisoners yielded a diary, some letters, a Colt service revolver, and a YMCA card identifying George A. Christian. All were charged with grave robbing and selling of bodies. As a result of the arrest and upon the recommendation of Dr. George A. Otis, Christian was dishonorably discharged from his government position. Physicians in the Washington area were harsh in their criticism of Christian both because of his far-ranging shipment activities and the recording of his actions in a diary. Furthermore, a reference in the diary led some prominent citizens to suppose that the body of A.C.H. Webster might have been stolen from Congressional Cemetery on October 29. Christian and co-defendant Charles Green were saved from answering for this last desecration. The charge was dismissed because of insufficient evidence. However, for the removal of Fletcher from Holmead's Cemetery both were convicted and sentenced to a jail term of one year and a fine of $1000. An appeal was made, bond being set at $2000.

The diary, in censored form, appeared in the *Evening Star*, a Washington newspaper. It resembles the diary of retired English resurrectionist Joseph Naples, published by James Blake Bailey under the title of *The Diary of a Resurrectionist* London, 1896. In it appears the detail of a professional grave robbing business, the like of which had not to that time been reported in the United States. The diary began on January 1, 1873. Following are the entries relative to the grave robbing and abortion businesses of George Christian from the December 15, 1873, issue of the *Evening Star*.

January 3d 1873 — B. and C. went out and got two cadavers tonight.
April 4th — Dr. C. and I went to the Washington Asylum Cemetery[1] tonight and confiscated two sets of extremities and one head.
Saturday 5th — There was quite a little excitement in this morning's market about our little adventure last night, many believing that another murder had been committed. No one suspected us.
Sunday, April 6th — Went out to Washington asylum this morning, and went through the institution with Dailey,[2] who was appointed resident student.
Tuesday, June 3d — Called on Dr. _____ to see about getting some tickets to Tom Wright's execution. Did not succeed.
Thursday, 5 — Received a pass from Dr. _____ for the execution.
Friday, June 6th — Went to see Thos. Wright hung to-day. Everything went on smoothly and he died by strangulation.
June 29th, Sunday — Went out to the Washington asylum this morning to see Dailey. He showed me around the hospital, and I stayed to dinner with him. Rode home with Dr. Schleimer.[3]

Beau Hickman's Body
Sept. 2 — Dr. _____ and I went out prospecting this evening, and succeeded in getting [characters in cipher, referring evidently to the body of Beau Hickman]. It was a lovely moonlight night and everything went off smoothly.
Sept. 3d — There was a great hue and cry in all the daily papers today

about the grave of Beau Hickman being robbed last night. Have not seen any one who seemed to know who did it.

A Resurrection Firm Established
Sept. 10 — Dr. Schlimer [note different spelling from above] called at the house for me this afternoon, and I rode out to the asylum with him. We talked about resurrecting next winter, and partly promised to go in together.
Sept. 11 — Called to see Dr. _____ at his office this morning in regard to furnishing material to his class for dissection. Dr. Schlimer called on me at the office to-day. We agreed to divide, giving him 8–15.
Sept. 12 — Called to see Drs. _____ and _____ in regard to furnishing material for dissecting. They were both agreed.
Sept. 18 — Called on Dr. _____ this morning, and he promised to let Dr. Schlimer and I furnish his college with material this winter at $15 each — we to inject and remove it.

The Doctor's Resurrection Money Comes to Grief
Friday, Sept. 19 — Jay Cooke and Co. suspended yesterday, and I was unfortunate enough to have some money in their hands. Went up to see about it to-day, but everything is closed and no information can be had.
Sept. 20 — Went out to the asylum this afternoon and staid until after dark with Dr. Schlimer. There was a cadaver on hand, but we could not get it. Went down town in the evening.
Sunday 21 — Went out to the Washington asylum early this morning and staid to dinner. Dr. Schlimer drove me around after dinner. We got a subject this evening.
Sept. 22 — Staid at asylum last night with Dr. Schlimer, and took breakfast there. Went to college this morning and injected our subject. Went out to the asylum in Dr. S. place to-night.
Sept. 30 — Got a permit from the Board of Health to-day to bury the material from the dissecting room of college. Did not go to the asylum tonight.

Business of Another Kind
Oct. 4th — Miss M called to see me professionally this afternoon. I gave her Tinct. Gentian, co.zi gtt der die.[4]
Sunday, Oct. 4 — Called to see Miss M this morning, and found her doing as well as could be expected.
Oct. 7 — Miss M came to spend a week with us this morning.
Oct. 8 — Got excused from the office for four hours to-day. Was sent for to come home and attend Miss M, who was suddenly taken ill. She had a miscarriage of a female child at 11 p.m.
Oct. 15 — Dr. Schlimer drove to the city this evening and took a subject to _____ College.[5] We got in just before the close of lecture, but got up quietly without being seen.
Sunday, 26th — We got a subject at Holmead's Cemetery[6] for College _____ to-night.
Oct. 29 — Attended a funeral at the Congressional Cemetery[7] this afternoon and brought the subject in to _____ College to-night. Called to see M to-day and found her doing well.

Feels Sleepy After a Busy Night

Oct. 30 — Was out until 3:30 a.m. last night on business for the College.
Felt rather sleepy to-day and had a slight chill this morning.
Nov. 2 — Went out to the Asylum. Took a ride out to
Glenwood Cemetery[8] and the Soldiers Home.[9] Took a cadaver in to
_____ _____.

A Disappointment

Nov. 3d. — Dr. Schlimer and I drove out to Harmony Cemetery[10] this
afternoon. Saw some subjects in the vault and went after them to-night
but could not get into the place as it was locked. Hazen[11] went with us.
Nov. 4th. — Tried to get Hazen to go with us this evening but he would
not do it. Dr. Schlimer took me down town to-night but would not go
anywhere.
Nov. 5 — Walked out to Piney Branch Hotel this afternoon, but did not
find what I went for. Mr. B and I went out to the asylum this evening with
Dr. S. and brought in a subject for N.B.

Not So Fortunate As To Meet a Funeral

Nov. 9th. — Sunday. — Dr. Schlimer went out riding this afternoon, hop-
ing to see a funeral, but were not so fortunate as to meet one. I waited two
hours near Ebenezar Church,[12] but did not find anything.

Out Prospecting

Nov. 10 — We went out prospecting at Rock Creek Church cemetery[13] this
afternoon but found nothing. We went to Holmead's this evening and got
a subject, which we took to _____ College. Got home before twelve.
November 11 — We succeeded in getting a subject at Ebenezar cemetery to-
night. Boardman[14] went out with me as Dr. Schlimer could not leave the
Asylum.

Two Subjects, Both Females

November 12 — Boardman went out with me again to-night and we got
two subjects from the dead-house at the poor-house. Took them to
_____ College. They were both females.

Another Female

November 13 — Staid at the Asylum last night so as to see Mike. Dr.
Schlimer, Stephenson[15] and I went out to Holmead's cemetery and got a
female subject for _____ College. Got through at 8 p.m.

Settling Accounts

Friday 14 — Called on Dr. Schlimer and settled for all but five subjects.
November 15 — I came home before 3 o'clock to-day and lay down. Dr.
Schlimer called just before dark, but I did not feel able to go with him.
Sunday, 16 — This has been a beautiful day. I stayed in the house until 3:30
o'clock p.m. when Mr. B., Mrs. B., Saide and I took a walk. We went
through the Congregational and Methodist[16] cemeteries.
Monday, 17 — I went out to the alms house in the evening, and tried to get
Dr. Schlimer out on a night expedition, but he would not go.

Found Things Too Wet
Nov. 18 — The rain of yesterday has turned into a wet snow storm. Dr. Schlimer called for me and we went out to-night but found things too wet.

Nov. 19 — Went out to the alms house to-day and stayed until evening, expecting to get a subject that was buried to-day. When we went down after dark, however, we found it not, on account of the darkness.

November 20 — Schlimer (M.D.) went to the lodge to-night, and left me to get the subject myself, which I did, and delivered to college dissecting rooms.

November 21 — Walked out to the alms house to-night, but our expectations were disappointed.

November 24 — I went to the Washington asylum in the evening, and went out with Dr. S. after a subject. We got one in Potter's field.[1]

Nov. 25 — Went out with Dr. Schlimer to-night to get a subject, but found too much work to accomplish, and abandoned it, as one came in this evening to be interred to-morrow.

A Handy Appointment
Nov. 26 — Dr. Schlimer was to-day appointed physician to the poor in the ?th district. We got two subjects in Potter's field to-night.

Dr. S "Red Hot"
Nov. 27 — Thanksgiving Day. — Stayed at the Almshouse last night and saw all the patients this morning. Did not get through until 10 o'clock. Came in and found Dr. Schlimer "Red Hot."

A Mistake About the Body of Henry Young
Nov. 28, Friday — Attended the execution of Henry Young to-day and took Mr. B. in with me. Dr. S. and I went to Ebenezar cemetery to get him to-night, but found a woman instead.

Nov. 29 — Received a letter from University of Virginia and Michigan, and answered them both; also wrote to Ossle[17] asking him to try and get me an order for subjects in Cleveland.

Nov. 30 — Dr. Schlimer and I got a subject for shipping to-night at Potter's field.

Monday, Dec. 1st — Shipped two subjects to Dr. Frothingham[18] to-day. Sent them in whisky barrels by express to J.D. Quimby & Co.[19] for him. Dr. Schlimer and I went to the asylum this evening, but got nothing. He gave up the keys.

Dec 2d — It rained a good deal last night. Dr. Schlimer, Dr. _____ and I went to Ebenezar to-night and found three new graves, but the ground was too wet to get them.

Cato to Get $2 a Subject
Nov (?) 3 — Got Cato, our janitor, to go out resurrecting with me to-night. We went to Ebenezar cemetery, but did not succeed in getting anything. We promised to pay him $2 a subject, to come out of Dr. S's share.

A Poor Nights Work
Dec 4th — Went to Holmead's and Young Men's Cemeteries[20] this p.m. Did not find anything sure at either. Hospital Steward Hilton was sent over to help me to-day.

Business Dull Again

Dec 5th—Wrote to Dr. Davis[21] this morning, promising to send him two subjects to morrow. Went to Holmead's and Young Men's Cemeteries this evening, but did not succeed in getting anything.

Dec 6th—Went out to the Alms House this afternoon. Did not find Cooper there. Cato and I went out to Ebenezar this evening, and got a subject, which we put in a barrel ready to ship.

Dec 7th—I went out to the Alms House this morning, and saw Cooper. Found Bennie at the house when I came back. We went out riding together. I got a subject at Holmead's to-night myself.

Monday, Dec 8th—Sent two subjects to Virginia this morning, and wrote a letter to Dr. Davis in regard to them. Cato and I went out to Mount Zion[22] to-night, and got a subject for N.B.

Notes

1. Washington Asylum, Washington Almshouse, Poorhouse, Washington Asylum Cemetery, Potter's Field—The Almshouse was located at 19th and "C" Streets, not far from Congressional Cemetery and the United States Jail. Potter's Field was located adjacent and immediately behind the Almshouse.

2. Dailey—??

3. Schleimer or Schlimer—Neither name appears in the Washington Directory for 1873. Schlimer may have been an alias.

4. Tinct. Gentian, co.zi gtt der die - Either a drug dose, tincture of gentian with zinc a drop a day; tincture of gentian, one teaspoon given drop by drop per day; or a code. Tinct. # with alcohol; Gentian # gentian violet; co # usually medical abbreviation for "with"; zi # possibly zinc, but more likely a cursive z with what appears to be an i after to indicate one teaspoon; gtt # an abbreviation for the Latin word meaning "drops" or "drop by drop"; der die # per day or this day. The later notation that Miss M miscarried a female child indicates that the pregnancy had to have been at least eight to nine weeks. The sex of the child is difficult to determine before this time. Based upon the information recorded here, Christian's reputation as an abortionist cannot be substantiated.

5. At this time, there were only four colleges in the District of Columbia; three of these had medical departments: National Medical College; Medical Department of Columbian University (George Washington University); Medical Department of Georgetown University; Medical Department of Howard University.

6. Holmead's Cemetery—Holmead's, one of the oldest burying grounds in Washington, was located on 20th and Boundary Streets. During Christian's time the Board of Health labeled the cemetery a "nuisance injurious to health" and directed that no more burials were to take place there. That Fletcher's body purportedly came from Holmead's is evidence that the directive was not followed.

7. Congressional Cemetery—Also called Parish Cemetery of Christ Church, Congressional Cemetery received its name because it was the final resting place for Senators and Representatives who died in Washington in the early 1800s. A number of other dignitaries were interred there, among them Vice Presidents Gerry and Clinton. It spanned several city blocks from "E" through "H" Street almost to "K," and from 17th to beyond 19th streets.

8. Glenwood Cemetery—Glenwood Cemetery, beautifully laid out and with many fine monuments, was located near the north end of North Capitol Street.

9. The Soldier's Home — Also located north of Washington, the Soldier's Home was for Regulars and volunteers who served in the Mexican War. It was financed with the money General Winfield Scott levied from the City of Mexico. The grounds comprised some 500 acres.

10. Harmony Cemetery — Harmony Cemetery was located at Fifth, Sixth, Boundary and "S" streets. It was a burial ground for free blacks.

11. Hazen — Possibly David Henry Hazen, M.D., (1846–1906) of Washington, D.C. Hazen was graduated from Georgetown in 1873, the year the diary was kept.

12. Ebenezer Church and Cemetery — Ebenezer was located between 16th and 17th Streets and "C" and "D" streets, near the Congressional Cemetery. It was a Methodist burial ground for blacks.

13. Rock Creek Church Cemetery — Rock Creek (St. Paul's Episcopal) Church with cemetery was the oldest in the District of Columbia. The church was erected in 1719, and remodeled in 1868. It was located north of Washington.

14. Boardman — Possibly Charles Vernon Boarman, M.D., (1851–1901) of Washington, D.C. Boarman was graduated from Georgetown in 1871. He served as a lecturer in the summer school of medicine at Georgetown in materia medica and therapeutics and was a clinical lecturer on diseases of the lungs, heart, and throat. In 1873, he was the demonstrator of anatomy at Georgetown. He also served as physician of the Central dispensary and city physician. His name was incorrectly spelled "Boardman" in the index of Atkinson: *Physicians and Surgeons of the United States* (1878). Name, time frame, location, and professional interests and activities indicate a possible connection between this physician and Christian. Other than the mention of a name in this diary, no solid evidence of a link exists.

15. Stephenson — ??

16. Methodist Cemetery — Methodist Cemetery was immediately opposite from Congressional Cemetery.

17. Ossle — ??

18. Dr. Frothingham — Although most of the physicians' names were censored out of the diary, this one as well as Davis and Dailey remained. Frothingham is a sufficiently unusual name that a reasonable guess concerning his identity might be made. We know from the letters Christian was holding that he engaged in interstate shipment of bodies to Virginia and to Michigan. His December 1 notation was that he shipped two subjects to Dr. Frothingham in whiskey barrels. George Edward Frothingham, M.D. (1836–1900), was an ophthalmologist and otologist who practiced in Ann Arbor. He was a demonstrator in anatomy and professor of surgery at Michigan University. In 1870, he was elected to the new chair in ophthalmology and otology, but he filled other chairs for brief periods as the University expanded and changed. In 1875, he was professor of practical anatomy. He quite frankly admitted to grave robbing and other illegal means to obtain sufficient anatomical material for classes at the University. Name, time frame, location and professional interests and activities indicate a possible connection between this physician and Christian. Other than the mention of a name in the diary, no solid evidence of a link has been unearthed.

19. Quimby and Son, Ann Arbor, Michigan — Quimby's must have served as a central receiving point for the collection of bodies as "Dr. Morton" also allegedly used this address for his pickle barrels.

20. Young Men's Cemetery — Free Young Men's Burial Ground, a black cemetery, was located at 12th and 13th Streets and "V" and "W" streets.

21. Dr. Davis — Christian wrote to Dr. Davis promising him two subjects, an

indication that he was not a local contact. On December 8, he notes that he sent two subjects to Virginia and wrote a letter to Dr. Davis regarding them. Davis may have been John Staige Davis (1824–1885) of Charlottesville, Virginia. He received his M.D. degree from the University of Virginia in 1841. In December 1842, he resided in Jefferson County, West Virginia, but in 1845, he moved to Charlottesville, Virginia. From 1845 to 1849 he was the demonstrator of anatomy at the University of Virginia and later became professor of anatomy and materia medica there. Name, time frame, location, and professional interests and activities indicate a possible connection between this physician and Christian. Other than the mention of a name in this diary, no solid evidence of a link exists.

22. Mt. Zion Cemetery — Mt. Zion, another black cemetery, was located near the 2500 block of "Q" Street. It was adjacent to the Montgomery Street Church, also later called the Dumbarton Avenue Baptist Church.

For murder, though it have
no tongue, will speak
With most miraculous organ.
                    —Shakespeare: *Hamlet*

MURDER!

No history of body snatching would be complete without some account of the murders committed for the purpose of selling bodies to medical and anatomy schools for dissection. Physicians who have written on the subject of cadaver procurement have characterized professional resurrection men as a callous and rough breed. There were several characters, who, by their actions, have exceeded even the horror engendered by the resurrectionists and have made history in the annals of crime. The most well-known of these are the Irishmen, William Burke and William Hare. Burke has the distinction of having his name forever fixed to this odious exploit.

Burke and Hare

William Hare, a peddler, and William Burke, a cobbler, resided in a lower class rooming house in a back alley of Edinburgh, Scotland. The house was run by Maggie Logue (variously spelled Laird, Log or Logue), a widow, with whom Hare lived and later married. No. 3 Tanner's Close in Portsburgh, or West Port, was a slum tenement. Logue owned three rooms on the first floor, two of which were rented out. They contained eight beds on which three or four persons slept each night for a few pence each. Burke, although married, lived there with a woman named Helen MacDougal.

The idea for a quick, easy way to make money was provided the four when one of the lodgers died owing the sum of four pounds rent for his room. Burke and Hare deftly exchanged the corpse for an equal weight of tan bark (so that the coffin would appear to contain a body) and peddled

69

the corpse first to Alexander Monro's anatomy rooms, and then to the unfortunate Robert Knox. The four "resurrectionists" realized a total of seven pounds, ten shillings, or a tidy profit of three pounds, ten shillings from the venture but found to their chagrin what the medical colleges already knew—that it was not so easy to produce bodies. Over the following nine months, Burke and Hare and associates allegedly murdered 16 people, usually by suffocating a drunken victim. Two of the bodies were recognized by Knox or his associates: that of Mary Paterson, a young prostitute, and James Wilson, a harmless retarded youth who wandered the streets of Edinburgh.

The activities of Burke and Hare were not halted by the medical men, but rather by Mr. and Mrs. Gray, friends of the last victim. The Grays reported to the police their discovery of the body of Madgy Docherty, a beggar, concealed at the rooming house. The trial lasted 24 hours through Christmas Day 1828. Burke and MacDougal were tried for the crimes with Hare and his consort supplying state's evidence in exchange for immunity from prosecution. William Burke was found guilty, hanged, and publicly dissected by Alexander Monro, Tertius. Helen MacDougal was released for lack of evidence (Barzun; *Lancet*, 1828–1829).

The fate of the other three conspirators is recorded by history. The mood of the public at the time was one of horror and they demanded legal retribution for Hare as well. It was with some difficulty that Hare escaped to England. There he secured employment as a plasterer's apprentice until his co-workers discovered his identity and threw him into a lime pit. As a result, he lost his vision and spent the remainder of his years begging. MacDougal eventually escaped to Australia where she spent the remainder of her days. Maggie Logue (Mrs. Hare) first traveled to Glasgow but upon discovery of her identity was nearly dismembered by a mob. She then boarded a ship for Belfast after which all trace is lost. There is some speculation that she traveled to Paris where she practiced nursing until her death.

Bishop, May, and Williams

John Bishop, John May, and Thomas Williams were all experienced body snatchers when they formed their alliance in 1831. Bishop, at 33 years of age, claimed to have been in the business for 12 years and to have resurrected between 500 and 1,000 bodies. May, who had some education and was a clerk, succumbed to drunkenness and lost his job. He subsequently found his way into body snatching as an alternative career because the hours suited him, the wages were excellent, and work was easy. He could also pursue his alcoholic habit without reproach since drunkenness was considered an occupational hazard. May was attracted to Bishop because of a clever outer-garment used by the latter to keep mud off his clothes while resurrectioning.

John Bishop and John May tried unsuccessfully to peddle the body of a boy to Mr. Carpus and Mr. Tuson at Guy's Hospital in November 1831. Refused there, the two conspirators next put the proposition to a dissecting room porter, William Hill, at King's College. Bishop settled on nine guineas. They departed to recover the body and returned to King's accompanied by Thomas Williams and another named Shields who carried the freight. Mr. Hill became suspicious when he viewed the corpse, which had a deep cut across the forehead. He suggested to Mr. Partridge, the demonstrator in anatomy, that the boy's death appeared to have been a violent one. Partridge concurred. In order to keep the four from departing, Partridge and the porter asserted that they only had a 50-pound note and would have to send out for change. The police were notified and arrests made. May avowed no knowledge of the body. Williams and Shields said that they were just along for company. The corpse belonged to Bishop.

It took some time before the body was identified as that of 14-year-old Carlo Ferrari, an employee of Italian beggar-master Augustine Bruen. Autopsy revealed that the boy died of a broken neck. His clothes, among others, were found buried in a yard at No. 3 Nova Scotia Gardens. More clothes were found at No. 2, where Williams lived. These proved to belong to a woman named Frances Pigburn, who had been about 35 years of age. Bishop and Williams were charged with her murder as well. With the damning evidence, a swift trial in December 1831 ended in the conviction of Bishop, May, and Williams. Bishop and Williams were sentenced to be hanged. They confessed to the murder of not only Carlo Ferrari, the 14-year-old boy, but also to that of two others — Pigburn, mentioned above, and a boy of about 10 or 11 named Cunningham. The murders were accomplished by a blow to the upper spine and drowning the insensible victims. These ruffians even removed Carlo's teeth and sold them to the dentists, a practice that was notorious among European body snatchers. Bishop in his confession noted, "I have followed the course of obtaining a livelihood as a body-snatcher for 12 years, and have obtained and sold, I think from 500 to 1,000 bodies." The corpses of Bishop and Williams were turned over to the Royal College of Surgeons for dissection (Cole p. 134–157; Packard, *Medical News* p. 72; Wright-St. Clair p. 69). May escaped the gallows and Shields, the porter, was never tried.

Torrence and Waldie

In 1751, Helen Torrence and Jean Waldie offered the body of a seriously ill, albeit not yet deceased, child to two or three surgeon's apprentices for dissection. The child was a boy of about eight or nine named John Dallas. Their plan was to remove the body from the coffin, substitute an equal amount of weight, and secrete their cache until the transaction with the surgeons could be completed. When the child did not cooperate by dying within a short period of time, the two women shortened the process by murder. In the absence of the parents (Torrence lured the mother to a local pub for a drink) they did away with the child and immediately sought out the surgeon's apprentices. Torrence concealed the body in an apron and carried it to the dissecting rooms. The two received two shillings and five pence for their effort (Cole p. 95).

Torrence and Waldie were tried and convicted in 1752. Both were sentenced to be hanged. The crime of murder was sufficient for the death penalty; but for the sale of the corpse, there was no punishment. That was not a crime (Wright-St. Clair p. 66).

Baltimore Burking

Since body snatching does not ever seem to have reached the levels of depravity in the United States that it did in Europe, Baltimore's burking case stands out as one of the few examples of criminality touching medicine. Even more surprising is that this event occurred in 1886, when most states had already enacted some form of anatomy law. It would be less astonishing, although no less appalling, for burkers to be encountered in the early or mid–1800s. Emily Brown's tragic story is described as it unfolded in the pages of the Baltimore *Sun*.

Emily Brown hailed from Easton (Talbott County), Maryland. She was a respectable woman from a well-to-do family. Her brother, Arthur Brown, worked for the Easton *Star* and when the paper closed during the Civil War, established the Easton *Journal*. The *Journal* was an eminently successful paper. Emily was a dressmaker and supported the children of her widowed sister with her talent for some 20 years. When her brother died, Emily turned to laudanum and whiskey. During the succeeding years, her addiction grew and her means diminished. She became a beggar in order to eat and pay rent. It was for cheap shelter that she went to Mary Blockson's house in No. 3 Pig Alley. Board was $2.50 per week and she paid from her begging. Unfortunately for Emily, she spent much of her lucre on her twin addictions and was therefore unable to pay the meager rent. By November 1886, she owed Mary Blockson $15.00.

Also living at the house in Pig Alley were john Thomas Ross, 28-year-old son of Mary Blockson by a previous marriage, Sarah Blockson, 11-year-old daughter, and Anderson Perry, about 50, a partly paralyzed assistant janitor at the University of Maryland School of Medicine. Anderson Perry and Mary Blockson were to be married on December 15. Albert Hawkins, who figured prominently in the murder, did not reside in Pig Alley. He was 32 and was said to have been involved in grave robbing.

According to Ross' confession, it was Uncle Perry's idea to do away with Emily Brown.

> Two weeks ago, Perry said to me, "If I was you I would make $15. You only have to work now and then, and you can make that much easily if you want to." I asked how, and Uncle Perry said, "That old white woman at your house — you could get $15 for her body." I said, "I don't understand; I can't do that"; but I met Uncle Perry that night on King Street and talked it over again, and we had frequent talks afterwards. I spoke to Albert Hawkins about it and we agreed to do it. On Friday [December 10] we went to the house and Hawkins staid [sic] outside and watched for the return of Mary Blockson while I went inside holding a brick hid in my hand. I said not a word to alarm the old woman, and while she was suspecting nothing, I suddenly struck a blow on her head, crushing her skull. I then went out and took Hawkins' place while he went in and stabbed her to make sure of it. We put the body under a mattress in the yard and went to the infirmary, and Uncle Perry asked, "Have you done it?" We told him what we had done, and he gave us a bag to put the body in. At 6 o'clock we borrowed a wheelbarrow at Joe's coal place, on Pig Alley. We put the body in the bag, laid it in the wheelbarrow, and in that way carried it along Dover, Paca, Lombard and Greene streets, and up Cider Alley to the infirmary, where Uncle Perry took charge of it.

The coroner's inquest added the details of discovery. Perry told Emil Runge, janitor at the University of Maryland, that a man had come to request the use of a wheelbarrow. Runge denied the request thinking the man to be a rag collector. Later Ross arrived with a body, warm, still bloody, and fully clothed. Runge, suspecting foul play, notified Dr. Hiram Woods, an assistant demonstrator in anatomy, who agreed that the death was suspicious. Dr. Woods directed his conclusion to the attention of Dr. Herbert Harlan, the University of Maryland's demonstrator. Dr. Harlan, upon examination of the body, notified police. Dr. Hoopman, one of the physicians who conducted the post mortem on Emily Brown, noted that in addition to the head and chest wounds, all the ribs on the left side were crushed.

Confronted with the evidence supplied to the police by the doctors, Alexander Perry confessed and named John Thomas Ross. Ross in turn implicated Albert Hawkins and Perry.

"The jury rendered the following verdict: That Emily Brown's death was caused on the afternoon of Friday, December 10, 1886, by wounds inflicted on the skull, and by incised wounds of the thorax, penetrating the heart. And from the evidence given we charge John Thomas Ross and Albert Hawkins, colored, with having committed the murder, and Anderson Perry, colored, with having been accessory to it" (Baltimore *Sun*, December 14, 1886).

John Thomas Ross was arraigned for trial January 22, 1887, in criminal court. His trial lasted only one day, going to the jury at 10:35 p.m. that evening. In 20 minutes they returned a verdict of murder in the first degree. Ross was hanged on September 9, 1887.

In his last written statement to the people of Baltimore, Ross, in poetry form, six stanzas, admitted his guilt but questioned the justice of allowing his co-conspirators to escape like punishment. The first two stanzas follow:

> Kind friends, your attention
> I'd ask a little while,
> And I'll tell you my misfortunes
> In my own illiterate style.
> Myself, with two more fellows,
> Who lived in this same town,
> For fifteen paltry dollars
> Did murder Emily Brown.
>
> I've no excuse to offer,
> My guilt I freely own,
> But does it look like justice
> I must suffer all alone?
> Is it fair, kind Christians,
> In this land of liberty
> That I alone must suffer,
> And the other two go free?
> (Baltimore *Sun*, September 10, 1887)

Cincinnati Burking

On February 15, 1884, in Cincinnati, Ohio, a one-story log cabin in the Avondale section burned to the ground. The house was inhabited by Beverly Taylor, 70 years of age, his wife Elizabeth, 55, and their granddaughter Emma Jane Lambert, 11. The little girl was adopted by the couple when her mother died. Murder was suspected by Marshall J.A. Brown when no human remains turned up in the ashes and no trace was found in a search of the immediate neighborhood including the dragging of ponds. The old gentleman, Mr. Taylor, was a rheumatic invalid and his wife took in laundry to support them. It was assumed that the motive could not have been robbery since the couple had very little worth stealing. Marshall Brown thought of the possibility of selling the bodies to the medical colleges and called at various medical schools to determine whether the bodies had been taken there. On Wedensday, he questioned Dr. Cilley, demonstrator of anatomy at the Ohio Medical College who denied any knowledge of the bodies. Upon giving further thought to the matter, Dr. Cilley then remembered that three black cadavers had been received there the night of the fire. The corpses, rather bruised and cut, had been delivered by two men, "Jack" and "Harrison." Dr. Cilley supposed that the condition was due to rough handling. The men received $100 for the bodies, no questions asked. Drs. Cilley, Kebler, and Walker, along with the coroner Muscroft, conducted a post mortem examination which revealed that the skulls of each had been fractured. Several blacks were arrested for the crime.

One, Allen Ingalls, was suspected to be a professional resurrectionist and allegedly had been active in the vicinity for some time. Ingalls was described as a stoutly built man of about 40 years of age. His most noticeable feature was "pop-eyes" with prominent cheekbones. The *Cincinnati Enquirer* said of him, "Ingalls does not seem to care what becomes of him, as he was frequently heard to say that he would not care if they killed him then and there. His dull, murderous-looking eyes protrude from their sockets, giving his face a revolting appearance that would put a hyena to shame. From his own statements he has for years been preying upon the dead for a livelihood. As his companion, Johnson, said of him: 'He is more like a demon than anything else when he is after a body.'"

Jeff Lout, a cousin of Ingalls' wife, was also arrested near the Ingalls house. He was described as a bad character with a brutal countenance. Fully six feet two inches in height, his occupation was given as plasterer. He denied any knowledge of the crime and submitted an alibi that placed him out of the Cincinnati area on the night of the crime.

Richard Ingalls, brother of Allen, was also arrested. He denied involvement in the butchery and murder.

The last of those arrested was Benjamin Johnson. It was Johnson's confession that led to his own and Allen Ingalls' conviction of the murders. Johnson aided Ingalls in procuring bodies from local cemeteries to be sold to the medical colleges for about $15 each. Johnson described the Taylor murders in his confession. "Ingalls told me the doctors must have some points on several occasions, and on last Friday morning he called at my room and said: 'Ben, I know where we can get three points to-night if you will help me.'

"I asked him where and he said: 'There's the Taylor family; they are no good for any thing else now, and we might as well have them.' I told him I did not like that kind of business, as I was afraid we would be found out. He said I was a coward and afraid to go with him and I finally said I would..." Johnson's description of the crime committed that evening is both vivid and gruesome. The bodies were loaded onto a waiting wagon and the cabin burned. Dr. Cilley was at the Ohio Medical College to receive the bodies and issue payment.

Johnson pleaded guilty to the murders, while Ingalls maintained his innocence.

Dr. Cilley's testimony is revealing of the activities of medical college anatomists and is reminiscent of that of Dr. Knox of Edinburgh. He stated, "There were three bodies brought to the Ohio Medical College last Friday night at about eleven o'clock, by the prisoners whom I identify. I was at the college at that time. They have been at the College before at night."

"Have they ever brought bodies to the college before?" asked the prosecutor. [County Prosecutor William H. Pugh]

"I decline to answer that question." [Cilley]

"Are they what are called resurrectionists?"

"I would so class them."

"How long have you known the prisoners?"

"I have known Johnson since last fall, and Ingalls four or five years."

"Were they at the college on the 15th of February?"

"Yes, at about eleven o'clock."

"What was their errand?"

"They brought three dead bodies."

"Did you see the bodies?"

"I did."

"What did you agree to pay for them?"

"I agreed to give $15.00 apiece for them. I gave Ingalls a 20-dollar bill the night they were brought to the college, and was to pay him the balance when he needed it. I assisted in the postmortem, and found that the skulls had been badly fractured. I am sure they met their deaths by violence. The prisoners, I am sure, are the parties who brought the bodies to the college."

A *Cincinnati Post* reporter questioned Dr. Cilley about the receipt of the bodies at the medical college. The interview was reported in the February 22 evening edition.

"You saw the bodies before you paid the men for them?" [Reporter]

"Certainly." [Dr. Cilley]

"And did you observe there were bruises about the heads?"

"I did, but thought nothing of it."

"Are the heads of corpses brought there usually bruised?"

"No, but they are sometimes caused by rough handling; but, my goodness! why, I never no more thought of anyone committing murder to sell the bodies of their victims than anything in the world, and it makes me shudder now to think of it."

"Is it not barely possible that you frequently buy bodies of persons who are murdered for that purpose?"

"No, I do not suppose such a thing ever occurred before."

"Yet, doctor, you would say the same thing to-day had not the mysterious disappearance of a whole family caused an investigation."

"Yes, that is true. I will say that it is possible that persons are murdered and brought to the college and sold to us. We never ask any questions, and our suspicions are never aroused by wounds as they may be caused by the handling."

"Then all these people who so mysteriously disappear may many of them land in medical colleges?"

"It is possible."

Such innocence, and ignorance, makes one wonder whether the medical community had learned anything at all about the causes of death from the many dissections they practiced. The demonstrator of anatomy must surely have recognized that the condition of the corpses belied natural death or post mortem mishandling. Murder to supply cadavers for dissection was morally reprehensible; the physicians who looked the other way, no less culpable.

A bizarre twist to this story is that the victim, Beverly Taylor, was also a resurrectionist before his physical disabilities overtook him. He lost two of his fingers from blood poisoning caused by handling "stiffs."

The law is the last result of human
wisdom acting upon human experience for
the benefit of the public.
                                    — Samuel Johnson

THE COMING OF THE ANATOMY ACTS

Although a number of states including New Hampshire (1834), Michigan (1844), and Connecticut (1833) recorded the passage of anatomy laws, most repealed them rather quickly. Only Massachusetts and New York had anatomy acts which addressed the provision of cadavers, criminal or unclaimed, for dissection by the end of the Civil War.

The passage of most state legislation was triggered by some cataclysmic event that forced legislative bodies to address the otherwise distasteful issue of human dissection. Following are some examples. The first is that of a riot in 1788 that continued for several days, drawing New York lawmakers' attention to the need for enactment of an anatomy law. The second is that of a Pennsylvania physician who found himself enmeshed in a body snatching and grave robbing scandal in 1882, some 15 years after his efforts had resulted in the passage of an anatomy act. The act was revised the following year. The third example is that of an Ohio congressman whose final resting place was to have been a dissecting table at the local medical college.

Resurrection Riot of New York in 1788

Activities of the New York medical program centered around King's, or Columbia, College, the first medical school in that city. Dr. Charles McKnight delivered the anatomical lectures for the college while private classes were conducted by Drs. Richard Bayley and Wright Post at the New

York Hospital building. Students who engaged in anatomy classes developed the ability to deal with the hideousness of the situation and as their familiarity grew, became hardened to the practice. Indeed, some displayed a cavalier yet jocose attitude toward their business. In early 1788, a series of letters began to appear in the *Daily Advertiser* from "Humanio," who abhorred the practices of the students in disturbing graves. Humanio's letters were rebutted by a "Student of Physic" who maintained that the public benefit was served by the grave robbing, specifically in the area of medical education and surgical expertise. The stage was set.

On April 13, 1788, some small boys were playing on the grounds of the New York Hospital. One of the medical students in the building exhibited more buffoonery than professionalism by waving a dismembered limb out the window at the children. The boys borrowed a ladder and peeked in the third-floor window from whence the limb was brandished. They saw, to their horror, corpses both black and white in various stages of dissection and dismemberment. They swarmed down the ladder and ran to tell their parents. The mother of one of the youngsters was recently deceased. Upon hearing his son's story, the father went to check the grave. We can only imagine the anguish this man must have felt when he discovered his wife's grave to be empty of all but her grave clothes. A riot ensued.

A letter from Colonel William Heth to Edmund Randolph on the 16th of April, 1788, reproduced for the *Bulletin of the New York Academy of Medicine* (December 1971), further clarifies the situation.

"The young students of physic, have for some time past, been loudly complained of, for their frequent and wanton trespasses in the burial grounds of this city. The corpse of a young gentleman from the West Indies, was lately taken up — the grave left open, and the funeral clothing scattered about. A very handsome and much esteemed young lady, of good connections was also, recently carryd off."

The mob stormed New York Hospital. All of the students except for Dr. Wright Post and three young men had departed. These few remained with the intention of protecting the collection of rare pathological specimens, one of the best in the colonies. Their efforts were in vain. The collection was seized and with other liberated bones and body parts was fed to a huge bonfire in the street. Post and the students were dragged into the street and would have met the same end as their collection but for the arrival of the sheriff and the mayor. The four medical men were placed in protective custody and escorted to jail. The mob, robbed of their intended victims, went in search of others. Prudent physicians and medical students escaped the city under the cover of darkness.

The next morning, the mob reassembled outside Columbia. Alexander Hamilton made an effort to dissuade the crowd from entering the college buildings but was pushed aside. They found nothing on the campus to arouse their ire and so again turned their attention to locating private physicians. The homes of Drs. Bayley and McKnight were fortunately devoid of anything interesting and the mob was forced to retire, yet unappeased, to local taverns.

Inspired by drink and accompanied by a new unsavory community, the mob gathered toward evening and marched on the jail where the physicians were still in protective custody. The city dispatched militiamen to secure the jail but these protectors were disarmed and chased away. The governor then called out the militia officers and swordsmen who marched on the jail. Several of the officers were wounded by rocks and other missiles. Col. Heth's letter names Baron Steuben, Mr. Jay, and General Armstrong as the victims. It was at this point that the soldiers fired into the crowd wounding several of the rioters. Heth's account notes, "...their might on the whole have been 60 guns discharged — but this is mere guess... Three of the mob were killd on the spot and one has since died of his wounds, and several were wounded. One of them was bayoneted on attempting to force into a window of the prison." Scuffling continued throughout the night, and with troops patrolling the streets, peace was achieved the next day (Gallagher).

As a result of the events of these early days in April, New York passed an act to prevent grave robbing in cemeteries and to provide subjects for dissection (executed criminals) in 1789. The "Act to prevent the odious practice of digging up and removing, for the purpose of dissection, dead Bodies interred in cemeteries or burial places" provided for the punishment of any person convicted of such action to stand in the pillory. Further, these persons were to suffer corporal punishment, fine, and imprisonment as the court should deem proper. Section 2 of the law noted, "In order that science may not, in this respect, be injured by preventing the dissection of proper subjects, that when any offender shall be convicted of murder, arson, or burglary, for which he shall be sentenced to suffer death, the court may, at their discretion, add to the judgment that the body of such offender shall be delivered to the surgeon for dissection" (Hartwell p. 218, 220, 224–225). From the date of passage, this law was inadequate. Not nearly enough cadavers were made available to meet even the minimum needs of the growing medical profession in New York.

It was some 64 years later, in 1854, that an Act to Promote Medical Science allowed unclaimed bodies to be given to medical schools for dissection. The New York Academy of Medicine recognized the passage of the "Anatomical Bill" by voting thanks "to the several gentlemen, professional and others, through whose agency the stigma hither to attached by law in our state to the study of anatomy and the dissection of dead bodies has been removed."

William Smith Forbes, M.D. and the *Jefferson Story*

Jefferson Medical College, as well as the other medical schools in Philadelphia, regularly received bodies from Lebanon Cemetery, a black burial ground, through a ring of grave robbers. The gang included doctors, cemetery caretakers, and professional body snatchers. Investigative reporting by Louis N. Megargee, city editor of the *Philadelphia Press*, and William Henderson, a Pinkerton detective, resulted in the ambush and capture on December 4, 1882, of a wagon returning from Lebanon cemetery with a cargo of six cadavers. Three men, Frank McNamee, Henry "Dutch" Pillet, and Levi Chew, were arrested. Two others were arrested the following day; Andrew "Yank" Mullen, the cemetery caretaker, and Robert Chew, the brother of Levi. Newspapers let it be known that the bodies were destined for Jefferson Medical College, but even more convincing evidence was Frank McNamee's (the wagon driver) possession of keys to several buildings at Jefferson including the building which housed the dissecting rooms.

The ring was charged with stealing bodies from Lebanon Cemetery. In the trial that followed, McNamee and Pillet pleaded guilty to hauling bodies but not to "breaking into graves." McNamee admitted to hauling bodies and Pillet admitted to employment by McNamee. The Chews both pleaded not guilty. Drs. Forbes and Lohman were charged with conspiracy and freed on $5000 bail. Dr. Benham was also named but he was not a state resident. McNamee, Pillet, Mullen, and Robert and Levi Chew were all found guilty of grave robbing. The jury foreman was heard to remark, "Is there no law to hang them?"

McNamee's statement was included in a local newspaper account and includes some serious revelations. He stated that Dr. Benham had initially hired him three years before to haul bodies from the prison. Later his duties expanded to include hauling cadavers from burial grounds for which he was paid $2.50. McNamee said that Dr. Forbes knew where the bodies were obtained. Forbes paid McNamee $1 for each body transported and between $5 and $8 to Levi Chew for each body delivered. As the business picked up, McNamee apparently had second thoughts, because he testified that he questioned Dr. Forbes about the possibility of getting into trouble for hauling bodies. On an affidavit from D.B. Bowser, Trustee of Lebanon Cemetery, District Attorney Graham asked that a charge of conspiracy to "violate the right of sepulture and to despoil graves in Lebanon Cemetery" be brought against Drs. Forbes, Lohman, and Benham. Judge Fell issued warrants.

The report of the hearing before Judge Fell concerning the grave robbing business by Drs. Forbes and Lohman followed. Charges were dropped against Dr. Lohman because of expiration of the statute of limitations. He had not participated in the business for more than three years. Dr. Forbes was bound over for trial.

Dr. Forbes, the author of the Pennsylvania Anatomy Act of 1867, was later acquitted. It was quite apparent that Jefferson had been for at least several years receiving illegal stolen bodies from Lebanon Cemetery. The lotholders of Lebanon Cemetery had their own meeting in which they deplored grave robbing in their cemetery and resolved to thank Louis Megargee for his work. They asked for prosecution of all concerned in grave robbing and an explanation from the secretary of the cemetery why 56 bodies were supposedly buried in one grave. A number of persons having friends or relatives at Lebanon obtained permits from the Health Officer to open graves to ascertain whether bodies had been disturbed. The repercussions of the burial ground activities very nearly ruined Jefferson and the other medical programs in Philadelphia (Philadelphia *Public Ledger*, December 6,7,8,14,15,16,18, 1882).

William Smith Forbes was born February 10, 1831, in Virginia. He was educated at Fredericksburg and Concord academies and studied medicine at the University of Virginia from 1850 to 1851, serving under Dr. George Carmichael. He trained at Jefferson Medical College where he received his medical degree in 1852 and was the office student of Dr. Joseph Pancoast, also of Jefferson. He was elected resident physician at Pennsylvania Hospital from September 1853 to March 1855. After serving in the English Military Hospital at Scutari during the Crimean War, Dr. Forbes returned to Philadelphia where he opened a private school of anatomy and surgery at Tenth Street and College Avenue which continued until 1870 except for the period of the Civil War. His military service included surgeon of the United States Volunteers, medical director of 13th Army Corps and surgeon in charge of Summit Hospital in Philadelphia.

In 1866, he received yet another medical degree from Pennsylvania University. From 1879 through 1886 he was professor of anatomy and clinical surgery at Jefferson Medical College. Among his writings are: "Harvey and the transit of the blood from the arteries to the veins per porositates" (1878; 7 pp); "The diaphragm; a protector of the heart and cardiac vessels; its influence on the organs of circulation" (1880; 9 pp.); "The liberating of the ring finger, in musicians, by dividing the accessory tendons of the extensor communis digitorum muscle" in the *Proceedings of the Philadelphia County Medical Society* (1884; 6 pp.); "The removal of stone in the bladder" in *Medical News* (1894; 10 pp.); "The removal of stone in the bladder at one sitting — litholapaxy" in *Pennsylvania Medical Journal* (1898); and "To make clean the hands and the field of surgical operation with a job" in *Pennsylvania Medical Journal* (1899). Dr. Forbes was the author of the Pennsylvania Anatomy Act of 1867 and perhaps his most important publication is "The History of the Anatomy Act of Pennsylvania."

HISTORY

OF THE

ANATOMY ACT

OF

PENNSYLVANIA.

BY

W. S. FORBES, M.D.,

Surgeon to the Episcopal Hospital, Member of the College of Physicians,
Member of the Pathological Society, Member of the
Academy of Natural Sciences, etc., etc.

PHILADELPHIA:
1867.

The title page of "The History of the Anatomy Act of Pennsylvania" by William Smith Forbes, M.D., 1867.

Forbes died of heart disease on December 17, 1905. Although not well known, he provided a great service to the medical profession for the practical education of young physicians. Because he perceived the need for legislation and succeeded in his quest to legalize the acquisition of cadavers and distribute them equitably, he contributed to the eventual demise of the practice of body snatching.

Two laws preceded the enactment of the Anatomy Act of 1867 in Pennsylvania. The earliest law governing illegal disinterment was Act No. 296 of 1849. It provided that no street, lane, alley, or public road should be opened through a burial ground or cemetery except that "this section shall not extend to the city and county of Philadelphia." It further defined grave robbing as a misdemeanor and "upon conviction thereof before any justice of the peace of the county where the said offense is committed, be punished by a fine, at the discretion of the justice, according to the aggravation of the offense, of not less than one (1) or more than fifty (50) dollars, ... and by imprisonment, according to the aggravation of the offense, at the discretion of the court, for a term not exceeding one year."

In 1855, the legislature again addressed the problem of grave robbing with Act No. 494, to protect burial grounds. This law enacted stiffer penalties for unlawfully removing a human body. "[S]uch person, upon conviction thereof, shall be sentenced to undergo an imprisonment in the county jail or penitentiary for a term of not less than one year, nor more than three years, and pay a fine of not less than one hundred (100) dollars, at the discretion of the court of the proper county." Vandalism of the cemetery or hunting within its limits was declared a misdemeanor and was punishable by fine of not less than five (5) and not more than fifty (50) dollars.

Not until 1867 did Pennsylvania enact an anatomy law that provided legal means to obtain cadavers for dissection. The story of Act No. 482 of March 1867, for the promotion of medical science and to prevent traffic in human bodies in the city of Philadelphia and county of Allegheny, also known as the Armstrong Act, was related by its author, William Smith Forbes, M.D., in his pamphlet "The History of the Anatomy Act of Pennsylvania." The complete text of the document appears in Appendix 1.

Dr. Forbes' "History" addresses several very important points that verify or reinforce the problems and or thinking of the mid–1800s. Owing to his experience as an anatomist, he had firsthand knowledge of the difficulty in obtaining human cadavers for the education of his students. He recognized that the study of anatomy was necessary to become a competent physician for, during his army service at Vicksburg, it was his misfortune to have come into contact with some surgeons who he believed lacked certain medical skills. He addressed the malpractice issue and its connection with the paucity of human bodies for dissection. Forbes noted that there were sufficient cadavers available in the city of Philadelphia, but that the law did not provide for their legal acquisition by physicians. The failure to provide a legal source of bodies opened the door for resurrectionists. Forbes alleged no fewer than three times that bodies resurrected here found their way to "distant States" and his law specifically mentioned that there should be no out-of-state distribution. Some measure of the legislative and public mind concerning dissection is seen in the reference to the proposed law as the "Ghastly Act." It is also apparent that Pittsburgh (Allegheny County) was included in the law very late in its formulation. It almost appears to be an afterthought.

Revision of the Armstrong Act came in 1883 with the passage of the Pennsylvania Anatomy Act, No. 106. It was enacted "for the promotion of medical science by the distribution and use of unclaimed bodies for scientific purposes through a board created for that purpose and to prevent unauthorized uses and traffic in human bodies." This law differs little in intent from the Armstrong Act except that (1) it applies to the entire Commonwealth, (2) it provides for the creation of a board, consisting of not less than five scholars, for distribution and delivery of cadavers and defines the duties of that board, and (3) it sets the penalty for trafficking in human bodies as a misdemeanor, if convicted, with a fine of not more than $200 and prison term of not more than one year.

The Snatch of John Scott Harrison

John Scott Harrison was the youngest son of William Henry Harrison, ninth president of the United States, and the father of Benjamin Harrison, the 23rd president. He was a congressman from Ohio. He died on May 26, 1878, of angina pectoris at the age of 73 and was buried on May 29. At the burial yard, Harrison mourners noted that the grave of recently interred Augustus Devin was disturbed and his body missing. Because of this discovery, extra efforts were made to secure the grave of John Scott Harrison. He was interred in a metal coffin and encased in cemented marble slabs. Grave watchers were engaged to guard the body.

John Harrison, son of John Scott Harrison, and George Eaton obtained the assistance of police and the next day began a search for the body of Augustus Devin. Circumstantial evidence led the group to examine the premises of the Ohio Medical School where they were met and escorted about by a janitor, one A.Q. Marshall. The search appeared fruitless and Harrison and Eaton were ready to move on when the police noticed a rope in a shaft. They pulled the rope and discovered that the body of an elderly man was attached. When they recovered the corpse, it proved to be young

Harrison's father, John Scott, stolen from the secured grave less than 24 hours after burial.

Newspapers discovered and carried the story even though the Harrison family maintained initial silence concerning the incident. Although Marshall, the janitor, was arrested on a charge of receiving, concealing, and secreting John Scott Harrison's body, which was unlawfully removed from the grave, no other guilty parties could be discovered.

The faculty at Ohio Medical College raised the $5,000 bail necessary for the release of Marshall but professed no knowledge of the incident. The dean of the college released a statement to the newspapers on June 1, 1878, indicating that under existing laws bodies for instruction of medical students were not available except by theft. He admitted that "the resurrectionist, unknown to us, who ... short of funds, took this means to replenish his exchequer" did exist but that neither the faculty nor Marshall was responsible.

In the face of public opinion, the remarks made by the dean, however true they may have been, were tactless. He drew attention to "resurrectionists" and incensed the Harrison family with this callous stance. Benjamin Harrison answered the dean in an open letter to the citizens of Cincinnati on June 3, 1878, which attracted further attention to grave robbery.

The court proceedings that followed revealed that a professional graverobber, Charles O. Morton, may have been the perpetrator of the snatch. He, assisted by his wife, procured a specified number of bodies for the Ohio Medical College each year. Newspapers reported that Morton acted under several aliases and had contracts with other medical schools. Finally, some of the faculty did admit that the college was under contract to obtain bodies for dissection. Cincinnati, it appeared, was the hub of a procuring and shipping operation. (Augustus Devin's body showed up in Ann Arbor.)

John Scott Harrison was quietly reinterred but his post mortem travels drew attention to the need for legislation to provide bodies and curtail body snatching (Sievers).

Ohio newspapers of the time (1878) reflected the tenor of public attitude toward the practice of grave robbing. There was no sympathy for the purpose for which the bodies were acquired, i.e. medical education of physicians. The writer of the following letter to the editor of the *Zanesville Daily Courier* even advocates a kind of vigilante justice for resurrectionists caught in the act. It is fortunate that cooler tempers prevailed.

> Surely, it is time something were done by the legislatures of our country to put a stop to this business. The punishment now for robbing a grave is little, if any, heavier than for robbing a hen-roost. Eastern nations have an imaginary demon, which they conceive preys upon the bodies of the

dead, that they call a Ghoul. But our ghouls are no imaginary demons. They walk about among us in broadcloth and kid gloves; physicians and surgeons, with lawyers to defend them, when caught at their obscene work; nice young men, who clerk in stores during the day, take their girls to places of amusement in the evening, and then replenish their depleted pockets by invading the cemeteries, putting hooks through the jaws of our deceased friends, sacking and carting away the bodies, and selling them to Professors of Anatomy for $25.00 a piece! This is horrible; but it seems to be true. The whole business of body snatching is becoming a systematized profession; and it will continue to branch out, and become a more prosperous profession, so long as the petty punishment for the offense is a poor six months in the county jail. Let not another Legislature pass by Ohio, without amending the laws for the protection of the dead. Let the penalty on conviction of grave robbing be from ten to thirty years in the Penitentiary; with this additional provision; that, if taken in the act, it shall be lawful for any one, policeman, sexton or citizen, to shoot down the ghouls like sheep-killing dogs. Then some good purpose will have been served by the present excitement of all classes of our people" [Edwards, Ohio Anatomy Law, January, p. 52].

The resurrection of John Harrison (or any other respected individual) was predicted by Sir Astley Cooper nearly 50 years previously in his testimony before the Select Committee of Parliament. The committee was appointed to investigate trafficking in bodies. Sir Astley was called upon to testify. The question was asked whether existing laws prevented bodies from being acquired and Sir Astley replied, "The law does not prevent our [the medical profession] obtaining the body of an individual if we think it proper; for there is no person, let his situation in life be what it may, whom, if I were disposed to dissect, I could not obtain." The committee next asked, "If you are willing to pay a price sufficiently high you could always obtain the body of an individual?" Sir Astley stated, "The law only enhances the price, and does not prevent exhumation. Nothing is secured by the law, it only adds to the price of the subject" ("Bodies for dissection" p. 381). Even though the scenes had changed, the script remained the same. Americans were slow to learn from their British counterparts. In this case and others like it, the anguish could have been avoided by the adoption of fair and equitable anatomy laws.

The first Ohio anatomy law was passed in 1870. Titled An Act to Encourage the Study of Anatomy, it became law on March 25. The abbreviated text of the law included:

Section 1. That it shall be lawful in this state to deliver to the professors and teachers in medical colleges and schools, and to members of county medical societies that are or may be auxiliary to a state medical society, and for said professors to receive, the remains or body of any deceased person for the purpose of medical and surgical study: Provided that . . . the remains shall not have been interred, and shall not have been desired for interment by any relative; . . . remains of no person who may be known to have relations or friends shall be so delivered or received without the consent of the said relatives; . . . remains of no one who shall have expressed a desire at any time that his or her body may be interred, shall be so delivered . . . remains of any person so delivered shall be subsequently claimed by any surviving relative or friend, they shall be given up . . . and it shall be the duty of the said professors and teachers to decently inter the remains.

Section 2. The remains shall be used for the purposes of medical and surgical study alone, and in this state only. . . .

Section 3. Every person who shall deliver up the remains of any deceased person, in violation of any or all of the provisions of the first section of this act, and every person who shall receive said remains shall, upon indictment and conviction, be fined in any sum not exceeding one thousand dollars nor less than three hundred, and be imprisoned in the county jail not more than six months. . . .

Section 4. This act shall take effect from and after its passage. . . .

It is apparent from the Harrison event that the law was unsatisfactory. The physicians of Cincinnati and Hamilton Counties recognized the deficiencies and, barely two weeks after the resurrection of Harrison, formulated a resolution to take to the state legislature to rectify the inadequacies. The text of the resolution from *The Cincinnati Lancet and Clinic* appears in Appendix 2. In addition to the proposal, several pages of discussion and debate among the members of the Academy of Medicine followed the presentation of the resolution. None of the views quoted opposed the spirit of the proposed revision. Indeed, one physician passed the following judgment on the then-extant Ohio Law: "The present Anatomy Act was so loaded with 'provisions' that it was practically useless. If, as Lord Eldon said, a coach and four could be driven through an act of Parliament, a whole army train could be driven through this Anatomy Act of 1870." It appears that the only disagreement was whether to actively pursue the passage of a new law immediately or to wait until the storm of public indignation died down. And there were differing opinions concerning the public attitude. Some of the physicians felt that the people understood the necessity for anatomical study and that the legislature would be more receptive to a new law in response to the preceding occurrences. Others argued that the public was prejudiced against the medical profession because of the recent attention given in the press to grave robbing. The entire debate was conducted without a single specific written reference to the Harrison resurrection.

As a direct result of that unfortunate affair the law was amended in February 1881. The amended version provided the following:

All superintendents of city hospitals, directors or superintendents of all city and county infirmaries, directors or superintendents of working houses, directors or superintendents of asylums for the insane, or other charitable institutions founded and supported in whole or in part at public expense, the directors or the warden of the penitentiary, township trustees, sheriffs or coroners, in possession of bodies not claimed or identified, or which must be buried at the expense of the county or township, shall, before or after burial by such said superintendent, director or other officer, on the written application of the professor of anatomy in any college which by its charter is empowered to teach anatomy, or the president of any county medical society, deliver to such said professor or president for the purpose of medical or surgical study or dissection, the body of any person who has died in either of said institutions, from any disease not infectious, if such body has not been requested for interment by any person at his expense; if the body of any deceased person so delivered be subsequently claimed, in writing, by any relative or other person for private interment, at his own expense, it shall be given up to such claimant; after such bodies have been subjected to such medical and surgical examination or dissection, the remains thereof shall be interred in some suitable place, at the expense of the party or parties in whose keeping said corpse has been placed. In all cases it shall be the duty of the officer having such body under his control to notify, or cause to be notified in writing, the relatives or friends of such deceased person; and any superintendent, coroner, or infirmary director, sheriff, or township trustee, failing or refusing to deliver such bodies he applied for, as herein provided, or who shall charge, receive or accept money or other valuable consideration for the same, shall be fined in any sum not exceeding one hundred dollars, and not less than twenty-five dollars, or be imprisoned in the county jail not exceeding six months; provided, however, that in no case shall the body of any such deceased person be delivered until twenty-four hours after death. The bodies of strangers or travelers who die in any of the institutions herein named shall not be delivered for the purpose of dissection, except said strangers or travelers belong to that class commonly known as tramps; and all bodies delivered as herein provided shall be used for medical, surgical and anatomical study only, and within this state; the possession of the body of any deceased person, for the above purpose, and not authorized by this section, and the detention of the body of any deceased person, claimed by relatives or friends for interment at their expense, shall also be unlawful, and the person so detaining said body unlawfully shall be fined in any sum not exceeding one hundred dollars, not less than twenty-five dollars, or be imprisoned in the county jail not exceeding six months.

Bodysnatching, resurrecting, night doctors was a pastime in which I was deeply interested and at one time engaged. There were pleasures and fascinations and excitements and risks attending it that were not found in any other phase of the study of medicine; but the passage of the Anatomy Act, in April, 1902, put a partial stop to the game; I say partial stop, for I believe that bodysnatching still continues. . . .
— Dr. Llewellin Eliot
Washington Medical Annals p. 247, 1916.

THE DECLINE OF
THE BODY SNATCHERS

By the late 1890s body snatching was a less common occurrence, and by the 20th century it had all but ceased. Many factors contributed to this rapid decline. Much as new scientific technologies change medical practice today, a new scientific technology was also responsible for this fundamental change. Embalming was introduced and became widely used. Cadaver storage and preservation improved thus drawing to a close the necessities of hasty dissection before putrefaction occurred. Cadavers obtained from legal sources could be accumulated over the period of time when classes were not in session and used as the need arose. Dissections could be performed with more attention to detail, in a less hasty fashion, and in a more complete manner. Although the numbers of medical students increased, the demand for bodies was not as acute as it had been before preservation methods.

Medical schools, once the victims of mob violence, had begun to command more respect as education improved. Indeed, medical education made great strides during the 1800s. A graded curriculum was introduced and more education was required for graduation. Gone were the old apprentice system, the diploma mills, and the sectarians. The emphasis of medical education shifted from gross anatomy to pathology and differential diagnosis. The medical imagination was caught by such subjects as growth and the aging process, hormonal derangements and endocrinology, immunology, heredity, and pathological physiology and histology. Evidence of the change in scope are the discoveries in anesthesia, antisepsis, bacteriology, and sanitation. With the new discoveries, the health of the population improved and the medical profession achieved a new esteem. Public support of the medical education effort resulted in the availability of a larger supply of cadavers (Norwood p. 422–428).

Organized medicine was coming to the forefront of leadership to achieve more equitable anatomy laws. Legislatures that chartered medical schools were being made to understand that fair anatomy laws went hand-in-hand with medical education. The days when a doctor was victimized for his attempt to gain knowledge by stealing cadavers, and concomitantly subject to malpractice laws if he lacked anatomical expertise, were vanishing. Physicians with newfound respectability were in a position to influence and enlist legislators in their cause.

Accounts of body snatching received less attention in newspapers. Possibly reporters thought that all bodies used by medical schools were obtained from legal sources. Perhaps grave robbing expertise had reached such a state of perfection that it was difficult to detect. In any case, with legal sources of supply on the rise because of revision in state laws, prices of illegal merchandise would have declined. As grave robbing became a less profitable enterprise, traffic in bodies also declined (Waite).

It did not disappear altogether, however. In 1895, Dr. Thomas Wright's Presidential Address to a meeting of the Association of American Anatomists included a reference to ongoing committee work on the procuring and using of anatomical material. He remarked on the social connotations of human dissection and deplored the practice of grave robbing.

> We anatomists, no less than others, shudder at the thought of the desecration of the remains of those who have been near and dear to us. The mad wrath caused by the feeling that graves are not safe is a well justified one. It is a disgrace to our civilization that in some parts of the Union body-snatching is still practiced, and that in others there exists an illicit trade in human bodies. Should any of my colleagues think me indiscreet in alluding to these matters, I must remind them that I am saying nothing which has not been made notorious through the public press.... I have alluded to the scandal of body-snatching, but an equally great scandal is its cause; the want, in many places, of an anatomy act, or the existence of one which the framers and all others know to be inadequate.

In December 1902, the *Medical Standard* reported the discovery of an extensive body snatching operation in the Indianapolis area.

> The authorities in Indianapolis believe they have unearthed a wholesale scheme for robbing graves in the cemeteries in and about that city. Twenty-five persons have been indicted for "body-snatching" or complicity in this gruesome business, among them several physicians connected with the local medical colleges. Some fifteen graves have been found empty and several bodies have been traced to medical schools and identified. It is

estimated that in the neighborhood of one hundred bodies have been
removed from their supposed last resting places by this gang, which was
apparently led by a number of negroes. The real responsibility for the unfortunate affair has not yet been traced to its source, though the citizens
of Indianapolis and vicinity are much aroused and may be trusted to ex-
haust the resources of the law upon the offenders.

With the report was an editorial comment that accurately reflected the
public view on the state of scientific and legislative advancement with
regard to anatomical teaching and cadaver acquisition at that time. "Grave
robbing, naturally enough, is regarded with especial horror and detesta-
tion, and professional men must look upon it with small measure of
satisfaction and approval. It was doubtless excusable, perhaps necessary,
a century ago — even less — when the law made no provision for anatomical
material, so essential to correct instruction in medicine. But there should
be no excuse for it now. . . ."

In 1895, the Association of American Anatomists conducted a survey
to obtain information about the collection and preservation of anatomical
material and the provisions of any existing anatomy laws. Their survey
went to professors of anatomy in 148 colleges in the United States, 25
foreign countries and 25 domestic and foreign medical journals. Forty-two
replies were received. The survey indicated that anatomical material was
gotten under the provision of the law in 30 states and countries; in part by
law, in 7; and without law, in 5. In response to the solicitation of information about anatomy acts, 10 considered the laws satisfactory, 10 found
them fairly so, 12 called them unsatisfactory, and 10 did not reply. The condition of the bodies when received was reported as satisfactory in 20 cases,
fair in 21, and bad in one. Physicians were much more forthcoming with
recipes for anatomical injection and preservation than their colleagues of
a century before. Many substances and combinations were reported along
with the cost of receiving and preserving the cadavers. The last question
concerned the adequacy of supplies for the purpose of anatomical teaching
and the number of students assigned to each subject. Fifteen respondents
said that supplies were sufficient, but that more cadavers could be used if
they were obtainable. Fifteen respondents stated that supplies were inadequate. The number of students per subject varied from four to sixteen.

By 1913, 39 states had medical schools. Only five states did not have
anatomy laws and three of these did not have medical schools. Alabama
and Louisiana had medical schools but did not have anatomy acts. Thirteen
states had an anatomical board in place which governed the acquisition and
distribution of cadavers. North Carolina and Tennessee still used only the
bodies of executed criminals for their anatomical supply to medical institutions. Seven states granted the use of unclaimed dead without any reserva-
tions for anatomical study. All other states provided for the burial of any

unclaimed dead at public expense. Mississippi and North Carolina prohibited the use of bodies of deceased Confederate soldiers to be used for anatomical study. North Carolina also included the wives of Confederate soldiers in its prohibition. North Carolina further refused to send the bodies of white persons to black medical schools for anatomical study. Twenty-four states, including Pennsylvania, Virginia, Ohio, Maryland, and Indiana, had laws prohibiting the transport of bodies for dissection over state lines. It seems likely that the states that experienced problems with interstate trafficking in bodies originally legislated against the practice, and other states not so exceedingly abused just borrowed the law. However, Virginia and South Carolina accepted importation (Jenkins).

In a survey of medical schools to review anatomical material received by them, Jenkins discovered that 41 schools were satisfied with the number of bodies supplied; 8 were not satisfied; 5 just barely; and one school noted that the supply exceeded its demand. Adequate supplies of bodies probably existed in areas where population was concentrated but less so in areas of low population density. The prohibition against crossing state boundaries doubtless worked to the disadvantage of medical schools in less populous states. Of those surveyed, most obtained their supply from almshouses. Some responded that their bodies came from distant points. This is reminiscent of the old boondoggle of "we get ours from anywhere but local." Thirty-four schools felt that the material they received was in good shape; five noted poor shape; and one claimed very fine condition. However, it was noted that many of the cadavers were autopsied before shipment to medical schools. Most of these would not have been very useful for viewing internal organ location or relationships.

In 1954, Woodburne published the results of a survey of anatomy laws in 39 states where medical schools were present. All states provided for the use of unclaimed dead; the disposition was determined in 26 states by an anatomical board or collective authority , e.g. Board of Health, and in 13 states, by an individual or small group. Unclaimed dead were defined as those bodies not assumed by friends or relatives for burial or those dead who would be interred at public expense. The time interval from death to surrender of the body (after a search for relatives) varied from 24 to 72 hours. Three states did not specify a time. Exempt from the law were the bodies of persons who requested a burial, bodies of travelers who died while passing through the state, and veterans. Virtually all of the laws dictated that medical schools or other medical institutions receive the benefit of the bodies provided by the laws, although more than half specified a waiting period of from 10 to 90 days before the body could be dissected. Woodburne found that prohibitions on trafficking in bodies were still in place in nearly all states.

The major change noted between the earlier survey and this is the legalization of directed disposal of the body, i.e. an individual could dictate the use of his body and or organs after death. The adoption of this tenet is a philosophical reversal of the old English common law that a dead body can have no owner and that the living cannot dictate the disposition of one's own dead body. The change in attitude paved the way for a new wave of advanced medical technology, that of organ transplantation.

Up the close and doun the stair,
But and ben wi' Burke and Hare.
Burke's the butcher, Hare's the thief,
Knox the boy that buys the beef.
—William Roughhead:
The Wolves of the West Port

POPULAR LITERATURE

Popular literature contains many accounts of grave robbing. The examples that follow show the wit and imagination of those who lived during the era when body snatching was at its height.

Doctors, Bodies and Snatchers

Hector Bryson's book, *Doctors, Bodies and Snatchers,* presents an excellent 19th century view of life in a university medical school environment. The story is of a young man, the son of a rural and relatively uneducated physician, who determined that he would like to become a doctor. He enrolled at his father's urging in the University of Edinburgh in the mid–1820s. The book details his search for decent living quarters, expenditures for books, and enrollment in classes. It seems that the young man came from a fine, religious family. Indeed, he arrived in Edinburgh affianced to the daughter of his local minister, an attachment he came to regret. He soon made the acquaintance of some rather questionable fellow students. Much of his entertainment centered on local pubs during the early part of his education. He engaged in one episode of grave robbing which went awry and determined not to expend any more effort in that area. His comments on the quality of teaching are similar to those of college students throughout the ages, but he found Dr. Robert Knox to be an excellent surgeon and anatomist. He somehow survived his medical school experience and returned home to accompany his father on rounds where his real education began. The interesting twist to the book is revealed in the young man's observations of his father's medical expertise. The university education he had acquired proved to be no substitute for the practical knowledge his father had attained through years of observation.

Bryson has woven the names of many of the great anatomists into his story, those of John Bell, Robert Liston, John Barclay, Robert Knox, and Alexander Monro, Tertius. His rendition of Robert Knox's introductory lecture to his anatomy course in which he sarcastically deals with his competitors is imaginative and believable. "'My aim,' [Knox] said, 'is to teach you some Anatomy and Surgery, and to help dispel the clouds of obscurantism that emanate from that canting humbug who calls himself Professor of Anatomy — Alexander Monro — Tertius.' He spat out the Latin ordinal as he might a piece of bad meat." The book also mentions some of the more disreputable characters of Edinburgh, Willam Burke and "Half-Hangit Maggie." Maggie Dickson was a criminal who had been executed. While the medical students and her friends and relatives wrangled over the body, Maggie came back to life although she never fully recovered her mental ability. She lived out the remainder of her days in Edinburgh and became something of a legend. Although *Doctors, Bodies and Snatchers* does not qualify as a landmark of literature, it does provide the background and flavor of the medical school environment of the early 1800s in England.

Marietta, or the Two Students

John H. Robinson's book, *Marietta or the Two Students, A Tale of the Dissecting Room and Body Snatching* (Boston: Jordan and Wiley, 1846), is scarce today. The plot involves the receipt by a medical student named Levator of a body of a young woman, Marietta, procured by local professional grave robbers, Gaunt and Thick. Levator found the woman too beautiful to dissect and returned her to the grave robber with instructions that she be reburied. Before returning her, however, Levator took one of the rings she was wearing and replaced it with his own. Instead of following instructions, Thick, the grave robber, sold Marietta's body to yet another medical student, Eugene. Eugene and his preceptor were engaged in experiments in galvanic energy, and the electric shock jolted the young woman back to life. When Marietta was fully revived, she resumed her former life. In a few months' time, Levator met Marietta at a social event where they compared rings. He, of course, realized who she was but she had no idea who he was. They married, thus drawing to conclusion a most bizarre tale.

Woven into the story is a theme that surfaces in other body snatcher fiction, that of prostitution. In Robinson's book, Thick operates his nefarious business out of a room in the madam's house. He prepares and stores cadavers in a trunk in the "dead room." The bordello is as low class as the grave robber himself and Thick meets his death in a fall from a rotted stairwell. Robinson spares no effort to portray the baseness of the grave robbers. Their physical description, their disgusting activities, the surroundings in which they lived, and their reprehensible behavior in dealing with the physicians and students permits no doubt of their depravity.

Ruth Sprague's Epitaph

A most entertaining epitaph which appears on a tombstone in the old section of Maple Grove Cemetery in Hoosick Falls, New York, reads as follows:

> Ruth Sprague, dau of Gibson
> and Elizabeth Sprague, died
> Jan. 11, 1846, aged 9 yrs., 4
> mos., and 18 days. She was
> stolen from the grave by
> Roderick R. Clow and dissected
> at Dr. P.M. Armstrong's office
> in Hoosick, New York, from
> which place her mutilated
> remains were obtained and
> deposited here.
> Her body dissected by fiendish
> Men,
> Her bones anatomized,
> Her soul, we trust, has risen
> to God,
> Where few physicians rise.

Although no "Roderick R. Clow" has been located in a search of the medical literature, it is unlikely that he was merely a grave robber. A record of a Roderick F. Clow does exist, however, and although he may not have been a physician at the time of the robbery, he later obtained a degree. He was a resident of New York and was licensed to practice medicine by the New York State Medical Society in 1847. His date of birth is uncertain, perhaps about 1830. He died in February 1878. Name, location, and time frame make Roderick F. Clow a possible candidate for participation in this resurrection, but no solid evidence of a connection exists.

Mary's Ghost: A Pathetic Ballad

A verse that is found in Gibson's *Rambles in Europe* has been titled both "The Invisible Girl" and "Mary's Ghost, A Pathetic Ballad." Sir Charles

Bell, a well-known London anatomist, purchased a house on Leicester Square for his residence and for use as an anatomy school. It was rather run down and he acquired it for a very small price. As it turned out, the house had the reputation of being haunted by none other than Mary, "The Invisible Girl." She was allegedly a beautiful young woman who was engaged to be married when she died. As the poem relates, she was dissected by more than one famous London surgeon (Haviland). By whichever title it is called, Thomas Hood's poem lends a light-hearted view to dissection and body snatching.

'Twas in the middle of the night,
   To sleep young William tried,
When Mary's ghost came stealing in,
   And stood at his bedside.

O William dear! O William dear!
   My rest eternal ceases;
Alas! my everlasting peace
   Is broken into pieces.

I thought the last of all my cares
   Would end with my last minute;
But tho' I went to my long home,
   I didn't stay long in it.

The body-snatchers, they have come,
   And made a snatch at me;
It's very hard them kind of men
   Won't let a body be!

You thought that I was buried deep,
   Quite decent-like and chary,
But from her grave in Mary-bone
   They've come and boned your Mary.

The arm that used to take your arm
   Is took to Dr Vyse;
And both my legs are gone to walk
   The Hospital at Guy's.

I vow'd that you should have my hand,
   But fate gives us denial;
You'll find it there at Dr Bell's,
   In spirits and a phial.

As for my feet, the little feet
   You used to call so pretty,
There's one, I know, in Bedford Row,
   The t'other's in the city.

I can't tell where my head is gone,
  But Doctor Carpue can;
As for my trunk, it's all pack'd up
  To go by Pickford's van.

I wish you'd go to Mr P.
  And save me such a ride;
I don't half like the outside place,
  They've took for my inside.

The cock it crows — I must be gone!
  My William, we must part!
But I'll be yours in death, altho'
  Sir Astley has my heart.

Don't go and weep upon my grave,
  And think that there I be;
They haven't left an atom there
  Of my anatomie.

Explanation of several of the references to names and places in the poem help to understand its tone. "Mary-bone" is probably an abbreviation of St. Mary-le-Bone, a large (for that time) burying ground in metropolitan London. "Guy's" is Guy's Hospital in London. It was founded by Thomas Guy and built during the last year of his life. It opened January 6, 1725, and did not achieve any notoriety until the early 1800s when Drs. Addison, Bright, Hodgkin, and Cooper among others joined the staff. These physicians have all left eponyms to modern medicine. "Dr. Bell" most likely refers to Sir Charles Bell (1774–1842), an anatomist and general practitioner. He is remembered for Bell's Law, Bell's nerve, Bell's palsy and Bell's phenomenon.

"Dr. Carpue" can be none other than Dr. Joseph Constantine Carpue (1764–1848), a pioneer in electrotherapy. His *Introduction to Electricity and Galvanism* appeared in 1803. "Sir Astley" is, of course, Sir Astley Paston Cooper (1768–1848), anatomist, surgeon, and practitioner. His name is famous for descriptions of Cooper's ligament, Cooper's hernia, and Cooper's fascia.

The Surgeon's Warning

Another poem revealing of the attitude in the mid–1800s toward body snatchers is part of Robert Southey's volume entitled *Joan of Arc, Ballads, Lyrics, and Minor Poems.* The poem, "The Surgeon's Warning," appears in the Ballads section and describes the impending death of a surgeon who, during his life, engaged in grave robbing and dissection. His instructions for the disposition of his body to prevent it from falling into the hands of body snatchers are contained in the verse, but all his precautions fail. In the last ten stanzas, the resourceful resurrectionists succeed in their attempts to bribe the watchers and secure the corpse. The story is reminiscent of John Hunter's quest for the body of the Irish giant, who also desired his remains to be placed in a lead coffin.

> The doctor whisper'd to the nurse,
>   And the surgeon knew what he said,
> And he grew pale at the doctor's tale,
>   And trembled in his sick bed.

> Now fetch me my brethren, and fetch them with speed,
>   The surgeon affrighted said
> The parson and the undertaker,
>   Let them hasten, or I shall be dead.

> The parson and the undertaker
>   They hastily came complying,
> And the surgeon's apprentices ran up the stairs
>   When they heard that their master was dying.

> The 'prentices all they enter'd the room,
>   By one, by two, by three,
> With a sly grin came Joseph in,
>   First of the company.

> The surgeon swore, as they enter'd his door, —
>   'Twas fearful his oaths to hear, —
> Now send these scoundrels to the devil,
>   For God's sake, my brethren dear.

> He foam'd at the mouth with the rage he felt,
>   And he wrinkled his black eyebrow,
> That rascal Joe would be at me, I know,
>   But, zounds, let him spare me now.

> Then out they sent the 'prentices,
>   The fit it left him weak;
> He look'd at his brothers with ghastly eyes,
>   And faintly struggled to speak.

> All kinds of carcasses I have cut up,
>   And the judgement now must be!
> But, brothers, I took care of you,
>   So pray take care of me!

I have made candles of infants' fat,
   The sextons have been my slaves,
I have bottled babes unborn, and dried
   Hearts and livers from rifled graves.

A police report from Edinburgh (1732) clarifies the previous stanza. "John Loftas, the Grave-Digger, committed to prison for robbing the dead! corpses, has confessed to the plunder of above 50, not only of their coffins and burial cloaths, but of their fat where bodies afforded any" (Kelly p. 201).

And my 'prentices will surely come,
   And carve me bone from bone,
And I, who have rifled the dead man's grave,
   Shall never rest in my own.

Bury me in lead when I am dead,
   My brethren, I entreat,
And see the coffin weigh'd, I beg,
   Lest the plumber should be a cheat.

And let it be solder'd closely down,
   Strong as strong can be, I implore,
And put it in a patent coffin,
   That I may rise no more.

If they carry me off in the patent coffin,
   Their labor will be in vain,
Let the undertaker see it bought of the maker,
   Who lives in St. Martin's lane.

And bury me in my brother's church,
   For that will safer be,
And, I implore, lock the church door,
   And pray take care of the key.

And all night long let three stout men
   The vestry watch within,
To each man give a gallon of beer
   And a keg of Holland's gin;

Powder, and ball, and blunderbuss,
   To save me if he can,
And eke five guineas if he shoot
   A resurrection man.

And let them watch me for three weeks,
   My wretched corpse to save,
For then I think that I may stink
   Enough to rest in my grave.

The surgeon laid him down in his bed,
  His eyes grew deadly dim,
Short came his breath, and the struggle of death
  Distorted every limb.

They put him in the lead when he was dead,
  And shrouded up so neat,
And they the leaden coffin weigh,
  Lest the plumber should be a cheat.

They had it solder'd closely down,
  And examined it o'er and o'er,
And they put it in a patent coffin,
  That he might rise no more.

For to carry him off in a patent coffin
  Would, they thought, be but labor in vain,
So the undertaker saw it bought of the maker
  Who lives by St. Martin's lane.

In his brother's church they buried him,
  That safer he might be,
They lock'd the door, and would not trust
  The sexton with the key.

And three men in the vestry watch,
  To save him if they can,
And should he come there to shoot they swear
  A resurrection man.

And the first night, by lantern light,
  Through the churchyard as they went,
A guinea of gold the sexton showed
  That Mr. Joseph sent.

But conscience was tough, it was not enough,
  And their honesty never swerved,
And they bade him go, with Mister Joe,
  To the devil as he deserved.

So all night long, by the vestry fire,
  They quaff'd their gin and ale,
And they did drink, as you might think,
  And told full many a tale.

The second night, by lantern light,
  Through the churchyear as they went,
He whisper's anew, and show'd them two
  That Mister Joseph sent.

The guineas were bright, and attracted their sight,
 They look's so heavy and new,
And their fingers itch'd as they were bewitch'd,
 And they knew not what to do.

But they waver'd not long, for conscience was strong,
 And they thought they might get more;
And they refused the gold, but not
 So rudely as before.

So all night long, by the vestry fire,
 They quaff'd their gin and ale,
And they did drink, as you may think,
 And told full many a tale.

The third night, as by lantern light
 Through the churchyard as they went,
He bade them see, and show'd them three
 That Mister Joseph sent.

They look'd askance with greedy glance,
 The guineas they shone bright,
For the sexton on the yellow gold
 Let fall his lantern light.

And he look'd sly, with his roguish eye,
 And gave a well-timed wink,
And they could not stand the sound of his hand,
 For he made the guineas chink.

And conscience late, that had such weight,
 All in a moment fails,
For well they knew, that it was true
 A dead man told no tales.

And they gave all their powder and ball,
 And they took the gold so bright,
And they drank their beer and made good cheer
 Till now it was midnight.

Then, though the key of the church door
 Was left with the parson his brother,
It opened at the sexton's touch, —
 Because he had another.

And in they go with that villain Joe,
 To fetch the body by night,
And all the church look'd dismally,
 By his dark-lantern light.

They laid the pick-axe to the stones,
    And they moved them soon asunder,
They shovell'd away the hard-prest clay,
    And came to the coffin under.

They burst the patent coffin first,
    And they cut through the lead,
And they laugh'd aloud when they saw the shroud
    Because they had got at the dead.

And they allow'd the sexton the shroud,
    And they put the coffin back,
And the nose and knees they then did squeeze
    The surgeon in a sack.

The watchman as they past along
    Full four yards off could small,
And a curse bestow'd upon the load
    So disagreeable.

So they carried the sack a-pick-a-back,
    And they carved him bone from bone;
But what became of the surgeon's soul
    Was never to mortal known.

Lucretia; or The Children of Night

Edward Bulwer Lytton (Lord Lytton) in his novel *Lucretia; or The Children of Night* (New York: Lovell, 1846), provides a macabre description of a body-snatcher, as villainous a character as one can imagine.

Gabriel Varney, seeking to consult a lawyer who resided in a dilapidated apartment house, found that he had to pass a second-floor apartment, No. 7, where, the porter informed him, lived a body-snatcher.

"He's a dillicut sleeper, and can't abide having his night's rest sp'ilt. And he's the houtrageoustest great cretur, when he's h-up in his tantrums — it makes your 'air stand on ind to ear him!"

And with that the body-snatcher opened his door.

"A huge head, covered with matted hair, was thrust for a moment through the aperture, and two dull eyes, that seem covered with a film, like that of the bord's which feed on the dead, met [Varney's] bold sparkling orbs."

"Hell and fury," bawled out the voice of this ogre, like a clap of near thunder, "if you two tramp, tramp there, close at my door, I'll make you meat for the surgeons — b-------- you!"

The body-snatcher retreated into his room and the young gentleman proceeded to his meeting with the lawyer. Upon the conclusion of business,

Varney again took the opportunity to bait the monster. As he passed the door of No. 7, he kicked it and sang out for the grave-stealer to come out.

"At the third shout of his disturber, the Resurrection-man threw open his door violently, and appeared in the gap, the upward flare of the candle showing the deep lines ploughed in his hideous face, and the immense strength of his gigantic trunk and limbs."

He succeeded in thoroughly terrorizing Varney. "The body-stealer's stupid sense saw that he had produced the usual effect of terror, which gratified his brutal self-esteem; he retreated slowly, inch by inch, to the door, followed by Varney's appalled and staring eye, and closed it with such violence that the candle was extinguished."

The Body Snatcher

Robert Louis Stevenson's short story "The Body Snatcher" is a fictional account of two medical students, Fettes and Macfarlane, who are charged with the receipt of and payment for material for anatomical demonstrations. Fettes lived in rooms above the dissecting theater. The students' teacher, K_____ is described as an "extramural teacher of anatomy," a popular and accomplished university professor. The man who bore the name K_____ "skulked through the streets of Edinburgh in disguise, while the mob applauded the execution of Burke and called loudly for the blood of his employer."

Fettes remarked upon the singular freshness of many of the bodies that he received. "The supply of subjects was a continual trouble to him as well as to his master. . . . [T]he raw material of the anatomist kept perpetually running out. . . ." However, he and Macfarlane agreed, "They bring the body, and we pay the price. . . Ask no questions for conscience' sake."

One night the resurrectionists brought in the body of a young woman named Jane Galbraith. Fettes immediately recognized her. He had seen her the day before and she had been in perfect health. When he called Macfarlane's attention to the situation, Macfarlane commented, "For me, you know, there's one thing certain — that, practically speaking, all our subjects have been murdered."

Later, Fettes found Macfarlane at a local tavern in the company of an unsavory character named Gray, who appeared to have some hold over Macfarlane. Two days later in the very early morning, Macfarlane delivered up the corpse of Gray to Fettes at the dissecting rooms. Fettes balked, but Macfarlane reminded him that "Mr. Gray is the continuation of Miss Galbraith."

Because of a shortage of material, the two students were called upon to resurrect the body of a woman from a rural church burial ground. The deed was done by raising the coffin and sacking up the body. On their long trip back, the nature of the cargo seemed to change and the young men stopped to check the corpse. It had been transformed into "the body of the dead and long-dissected Gray."

The Stevenson tale is revealing in that K_____ appears to be the famous English anatomist, Robert Knox, who had the misfortune of buying the bodies of murdered individuals from Burke and Hare. MacFarlane may have been Robert Liston, a very well-known surgeon of the period, who was a resurrectionist during his student days. The unfortunate Knox is depicted as a villain, and his students, totally without moral standards. Neither of these allegations has substance. Much of the damage to Knox's reputation occurred at the hands of newspapers, who vilified him first and asked questions after; his rivals, who sought to gain advantage for their schools at his expense; and the public, who were religiously critical of his practices. To some extent, Knox's own personality contributed to his downfall. Cole (p. 110–111) describes him as arrogant and unlovable. He had blue eyes, one of which was destroyed by smallpox. He was prematurely bald and curled the fringe of his thin blonde hair with his sister's curling iron. "His mouth and nose were big and his cheeks pock-marked; his taste in dress was more showy than that of any resurrectionist: a puce coat, dark trousers and highly polished boots; a tall cravat, often brightly striped, passed through a diamond ring; a bright waistcoat, embroidered with purple, and festooned with gold chains and seals; his fingers sparkling with diamonds. Like most arrogant men, he would never admit a mistake, was frequently evasive and often lied. His lectures were peppered with sneers at rival teachers and he was immoderately jealous of them." His assistants, who received the bodies, were very young and did not have the advantage of medical experience necessary to determine cause of death.

The story is entertaining even though the details are inaccurate.

The Wolves of the West Port

The Wolves of the West Port by William Roughhead is a report of the crimes of Burke and Hare related with the skill of an experienced storyteller. Roughhead was an Edinburgh lawyer who consulted the records of the criminal courts to obtain the fodder for many of his chronicles. The introduction to the subject of this narrative is a small square of leather, purportedly a piece of the preserved hide of William Burke, purchased and passed down through three generations of the writer's family. Even though the owner is proud of his small possession, he mentioned that some others had larger lots of the material, and that one individual had enough to make a tobacco pouch. *Wolves* covers the murders of Burke and Hare one by one with considerable attention to details until the pair were eventually discovered by the Grays. The arrest, trial, conviction, execution and public dissection of Burke by Alexander Monro follow the historical record very accurately. Even the story of Burke's lament from his prison cell for his lost fee from Dr. Knox for the body of the Docherty woman is reported. The last section is devoted to the life of Robert Knox with comments and descriptions taken from Knox's biographer, Lonsdale, and from Sir Robert Christison. Roughhead delves into the character and appearance of the man who played such a dramatic role in the Edinburgh "burking" scandals. Today we debate rather dispassionately whether Knox was a victim or an accomplice. The people of Edinburgh had made their decision.

Court of Cacus

Writing 30-plus years after the crimes, Alexander Leighton produced an engrossing account of the activities of Burke, Hare, McDougal, and Log in *Court of Cacus or, The Story of Burke and Hare*. Although written from the point of view of an intelligent observer, the book contains enough descriptive detail on the individual actors and the technique of the murders that the flavor of the times and the horror of the body selling scheme reach out of the pages. The early chapters deal with the true body snatchers and include some stories of Andrew Merrilees and his confederates. Mention is made of some of the great surgical anatomy teachers of the day. Chief among them was Robert Knox, later to play a role in the receipt of murdered corpses, whose physical description included a reference to "a blind eye resembling a grape" and his personality, that of "rampant egotism." Others such as Robert Liston and Alexander Monro receive comment. After a brief chapter on the importance of a cooperative effort among church sextons, relatives, and physicians in obtaining fresh corpses for the anatomy classes, the tale of Burke and Hare began. Leighton emphasized that the two were thoroughly degenerate, devoid of pity, and driven to murder for the money only. As the story of each new victim unfolded, the moral commentary became more critical and creative. The pair were at one point described as "dipsomaniacs in blood." Speculation . . . is that Burke and Hare murdered many more people than they confessed. It is probable that these untraced corpses were the street people of Edinburgh. It is further supposed that had the activities of this despicable duo been confined to the homeless, they might have gone on undetected for years. They did not confine their murders to unknowns however, and first aroused suspicion with the murder of Mary Paterson, an 18-year-old prostitute whose remains were recognized by Knox's assistants. The second error was the murder of well-known James Wilson, or Daft Jamie, about which Leighton remarked, "This was beyond all question the most imprudent of all the acts of these terrible beings." Not only did Knox's assistants recognize Jamie, but his clothes were distributed to relatives of Burke and Hare, and they too were recognized.

Leighton emphasized the lack of evidence to convict the four of the crimes with which they were accused. There were no witnesses, and no bodies. Had not Hare and his wife plea bargained, the case against Burke could not have been mustered. Burke himself never repented. Indeed, he asked for payment for the last body delivered to Dr. Knox so that he might buy a suit to look more respectable. He resented his conviction and Hare's freedom. Denouement of *The Court of Cacus* traced the remaining three characters in as far as their fate was known or supposed.

In one of the last chapters of the book, the behavior of the doctors was examined especially in regard to recognition of some of the victims and the obvious fresh, but damaged, condition of the corpses upon delivery. Leighton failed to advance the philosophical excuse so often mouthed for the doctors' behavior, that of scientific advancement for the benefit of humanity. The complicity with which the medical students and anatomical demonstrators dealt with body snatchers or even the murderers, Burke and Hare, grew out of the same motive that generated the trade, that of money. He maintained that the medical students had a strong wish for subjects, which stemmed from a wish for knowledge, which was in turn generated by a desire for money. Even if they did not *know* the conditions under which the bodies were delivered to them, they did at least suspect.

Court of Cacus parallels much of the information published in *Burke and Hare: The Resurrection Men; A Collection of Contemporary Documents Including Broadsides, Occasional Verses, Illustrations, Polemics, and a Complete Transcript of the Testimony at the Trial* edited by Jacques Barzun. The story closely follows the transcript of the trial; thus, the skeletal framework of the book is grounded in fact. Some of the descriptive material is perhaps fanciful, but not beyond the realm of possible.

The Anatomist and The Doctor and the Devils

Two plays, *The Anatomist* by James Bridie (pseudonym) and *The Doctor and the Devils* by Dylan Thomas, re-enact the business of Burke and Hare. Bridie's, published first in 1931, is subtitled "A Lamentable Comedy of Knox, Burke and Hare and the West Port Murders." While many of the characters retain the names of historical personalities, the play is not intended to be an accurate or serious representation of the events of 1828.

Thomas' screenplay, on the other hand, is a solemn drama that addresses sin, guilt, and death. The characters, Rock, Fallon, and Broom, are thinly disguised versions of their true-to-life counterparts, Knox, Burke, and Hare. The scene descriptions interspersed throughout the dialog evoke, vividly, the feeling of poverty, squalor, and depravity. Although the subject of both plays is the same, the approach of the two playwrights is strikingly different.

A Tale of Two Cities

Dickens' *A Tale of Two Cities* contains reference to the activities of body snatchers in a chapter entitled "The Honest Tradesman." The story opens with Jerry Cruncher and his son, Young Jerry, idling on a street-corner. A funeral procession passes, and the cortege is mobbed. The hearse is opened and the coffin removed to make room for the mob to ride. Cruncher joined the fray and accompanied the crowd to the burial ground where the body was properly disposed.

Cruncher remained behind in the churchyard while the mob turned to looting and other pursuits. On his return, he made a stop at the local surgeon's. Then, Cruncher and son went home to tea, where he announced to his wife that he planned to go "fishing" during the night and do the work of an "honest tradesman." He started his excursion at about 1:00 a.m. and took with him a sack, crowbar, rope, chain, and "other fishing tackle of that nature."

Young Jerry, intent upon finding out about the honest calling, followed his father. He observed that the elder Cruncher was met by two other fishermen and that they proceeded to the local graveyard. "They fished with a spade, at first." Then they used a corkscrew-shaped implement. Eventually, the three raised the coffin from the ground and proceeded to pry it open. Young Jerry became so frightened that he ran all the way home.

To be expected, "there was no fish for breakfast..."

As Cruncher and his son set out for the day's work, young Jerry asked, "Father, what's a Resurrection-Man?"

Cruncher replied that a Resurrection-man was a tradesman.

Whereupon Jerry asked, "What's his goods, father?"

Cruncher made an evasive reply and his son then commented, "Person's bodies, ain't it, father?"

When Cruncher allowed that it was, Jerry replied, "Oh, father, I should so like to be a Resurrection-Man when I'm quite growed up."

The elder Cruncher in Dickens' story is a rascal, a wife abuser, and very probably a loafer as well. The resurrection work turned an excellent profit for a small effort, a trade well-suited to Cruncher's character. The details of the story are inaccurate but the portrayal of the grave robber's personal qualities seem in keeping with the attributes that have been assigned them.

The Life of Mansie Wauch

The Life of Mansie Wauch, Tailor in Dalkeith, written by himself and edited by D.M. Moir, is a first person account of life in Scotland during the 1800s. The book is a fictional autobiography in Scottish dialect and is difficult to read. It differs markedly from the other popular literature of the period that mentions grave robbers in that this account presents the feeling of the townspeople toward desecration of their burial grounds. The local citizens of Dalkeith organized to stand watches in the cemetery when it was discovered that the graves of their friends and relatives were opened and the bodies missing. The argument that doctors and medical students needed dead bodies to learn to treat the living was given little credence. Indeed, the townspeople felt that the remedy was worse than the disease.

Mansie, by then a young man, was paired with a lad of 13 to stand the watch on a bleak November night. Carrying a flask and a borrowed gun from a neighbor, the two settled down to a thoroughly hair-raising experience. Much of their fright was caused by their own imaginations, night noises in the graveyard, and the visit of the village half-wit who regaled them with stories of ghosts, Irish medical students and grave robbers. Mansie became so overcome that he fainted when the cork popped out of the ale flask because it was too close to the chimney.

Summary

The popular or fictional literature represents one of the few remaining records, fanciful or not, of an era that played an important part in the growth and development of modern medicine. The tales described here (and others probably buried) furnish colorful particulars of an unremembered era of our history. They serve as a reminder that there is a skeleton in almost every closet.

Appendixes

A: "History of the Anatomy Act of Pennsylvania"

by William Smith Forbes, M.D., 1867

At a stated meeting of the College of Physicians held February 6th, 1867, Doctor W.S. Forbes offered the following resolution:

"Resolved, That a Committee of three be appointed to present the views of this College to the Legislature of the State urging the passage of a law sanctioning the dissecting of dead human bodies."

He said: "In presenting this resolution and asking its adoption by the college, it may be proper to state how legislative enactment, authorizing and regulating dissecting, will enhance the cultivation of the study of anatomy.

"Two considerations present themselves at the very threshold of the matter. One is general in its nature, representing the broad catholic principle of being right in itself, and embraces the very root of everything that is accurate, and useful, and learned in medicine. The other is entirely in its character, and interesting to us as physicians of a great medical metropolis. Both of them gravely appeal to this body for sanction in its highest corporate capacity, and both of them impel us to ask for legislative action.

"In regard to the first consideration, that of its being right in itself, I am free to confess, in this learned body it would be out of place to do more than announce so manifest a statement.

"I shall therefore address myself at once to the examination of the remaining consideration, namely, that of its being interesting to us as physicians of Philadelphia. And I trust it may not be thought impertinent in me to state, by way of preface, that after having been a teacher of anatomy and operative surgery in this city for ten years, to classes numbering in the aggregate near a thousand students, some of them now within the sound of my voice, I may be supposed to know something of the difficulties in the way of obtaining sufficient material for purposes of practically teaching so large a number of young gentlemen.

"In view of the fact that our city contains now three-quarters of a million inhabitants, I think it is idle to suppose there is not ample number of unclaimed dead bodies to satisfy the demands of all who may come for the purpose of cultivating a knowledge of anatomy, both healthy and morbid. In what then is the difficulty?

"I believe it consists entirely in the fact that as there is no law of the Commonwealth by which our physicians can claim these dead bodies, to be used for medical investigation, the authorities in whose hands they are lodged do not feel themselves at liberty to give them up for any purpose, however laudable.

"They are therefore buried, and are afterward obtained surreptitiously by a third party, the so-called 'resurrectionists,' who engage in a degrading traffic, and sell them to the highest bidder, as it is well known that the anatomists of medical schools in distant states send here every winter to supply their dissecting rooms, the debasing trade is stimulated, and the practical teachers here and elsewhere find themselves in unworthy competition with each other. Consequently, the price demanded, and often obtained, is such as to tempt the resurrectionist to enter private cemeteries and graves, and even to commit murder, as was the case in Edinburgh, in 1829. All tending to bring obloquy in anatomical teaching, to deter the student from pursuing his studies with that degree of diligence which is requisite for his future usefulness, and to the injury of our city as a seat of medical learning.

"During the rebellion, when a surgeon of volunteers, and particularly as Medical Director of the 13th Army Corps, U.S. Volunteers, before and during the siege of Vicksburg, in 1863, I had ample opportunities of being a painful witness in observing the want of a practical knowledge of anatomy, on the part of many surgeons. And I can attribute this ignorance only to the obstacles in the way of having freely and systematically dissected the dead body during their novitiate and afterwards.

"Believing this to be the case, and with the view of removing one very great difficulty, I drew up the following 'Act,' and submitted it last winter to the Legislature of the State:

"'An Act for the Promotion of Medical Science, and to prevent the Traffic in Human Bodies.

"'Section 1. Be it enacted by the Senate and House of Representatives of the Commonwealth of Pennsylvania in General Assembly met, and it is hereby enacted by the authority of the same, That the Inspectors and Superintendent of any county prison, the Board of Guardians of any City or County Almshouse, the Coroner of any County, or any other public officer having charge thereof, or control over the same, shall give permission to any physician, or surgeon, of the same county, upon his request made therefor, to take the bodies of such persons dying in such prison, almshouse, or county, as are required to be buried at public expense, to be by him used, within the state, for the advancement of medical science, preference being given to Medical Schools, public and private; and said bodies to be distributed to and among the same equitably, the number assigned to each being proportioned to that of its students; Provided, however, That if the deceased person, during his or her last sickness, of his or her own accord, shall request to be buried, or if any person, claiming to be, and satisfying the proper authorities that he is, of kindred to the deceased, shall ask to have the body for burial, it shall be surrendered for interment, or if such deceased person was a stranger or traveler, who died suddenly, the body shall be buried, and shall not be handed over as aforesaid.

"'Section 2. Every physician or surgeon, before receiving any such dead body, shall give to the proper authorities, surrendering the same to him, a sufficient bond that such body shall be used only, for the promotion of medical science, within this state, and whosoever shall use such body, or bodies, for any other purpose, or shall remove the same beyond the limits of this state, and whosoever shall sell, or buy, such body, or bodies, or in any way traffic in the same, shall be deemed guilty of a misdemeanor, and shall, on conviction, be imprisoned for a term not exceeding five years, at hard labor, in the county jail.'

"This Act passed the House of Representatives, but in the Senate a member objected to it as being unworthy of the age in which we live, and as his influence was of weight in that assembly, it was thought proper to withdraw the 'Act' until a more propitious time.

"In view of which I now desire to have the sanction of this body, believing that coming from such high authority, and exerted in so just a cause, there can be but one issue to the event."

The resolution was duly submitted, and the college unanimously passed it.

The committee appointed were Dr. W.S. Forbes, Dr. S.D. Gross, Dr. D. Hayes Agnew.

At a stated meeting of the College of Physicians held April 3d, 1867, Doctor Forbes, chairman of the committee appointed to present the views of the college to the Legislature of the State, urging the passage of a law sanctioning the dissecting of dead human bodies, read the following report:

"Mr. President: The committee appointed to present the views of this college to the Legislature of the State, urging passage of a law sanctioning the dissecting of dead human bodies, respectfully report that they convened, and concluded to express the views of the college in the form of a statutory act, and ask that it be made a law. Accordingly, the paper drawn up, and read, and shown to the college by the mover of the resolution, appointing this committee on the 6th of February, entitled "An Act for the Promotion of Medical Science, and to prevent the traffic in human bodies," was approved and placed in the hands of Senator Wilmer Worthington, of Chester, a doctor of medicine, and a gentleman whose high character and influence materially advanced our cause, with the request that he would read it in place, and ask its passage by the Senate. This Act provides that the bodies of all persons to be buried at the public expense shall be given to any physician or surgeon of the same city or county claiming them for the promotion of medical science; and that an equitable distribution of these bodies shall be made, preference being given to medical schools, public and private; and that they shall in no case be taken out of the State, and that no traffic in them whatsoever shall exist. The Senate referred the Act to a committee, which adopted a negative report, and presented it the following day. Senator Worthington then asked the Senate to recommit the Act, and that permission be granted the college committee to appear and explain their views.

"Your committee determined to proceed to Harrisburg for this purpose and as one of their number, Dr. Gross, was unable, from professional and other engagements, to accompany them, Dr. Henry Hartshorne was invited to unite with and assist them in their endeavors. Dr. Hartshorne consented, and your committee would acknowledge his services.

"Your committee found the legislative mind opposed to the passage of our Act, and it became necessary to explain its virtues with becoming care, for it was called a 'Ghastly Act' with more temper than wisdom, by leading representatives.

"It was submitted that the Legislature had granted charters to a number of medical institutions which based their instruction on a knowledge of anatomy, and yet there was no law permitting the examination of the human body. That in the courts of the Commonwealth the physician was liable to be arraigned for malpractice, in cases of accident requiring surgical treatment, and yet he was debarred from obtaining the very knowledge he was required to display under heavy penalties.

"That owing to the absence of such a law as was now presented for their sanction, giving all unclaimed dead bodies to the medical institutions, the price demanded and obtained by the degraded and debased creatures who engage in the traffic, known as the resurrectionists, became a temptation to commit murder, as in the case of Burke, who at Edinburgh, in 1829, slew fifteen innocent human beings, for the purpose, as he confessed at his trial, of obtaining four guineas from the medical schools.

"That it was only when the cause of this dreadful crime became known the British Parliament, in view of the necessity of anatomical investigation, passed the so-called Warburton Act, which was founded in a measure to subserve the purposes for which it was intended.

"That graves and private cemeteries were entered, and the dead bodies brought to the dissecting-table here, and frequently sent to distant cities for purposes of anatomical instruction, were often sought after by sorrowing friends much to the chagrin of the anatomist, and maledictions applied to his pursuit.

"These, with other arguments, were advanced, and finally, it was gravely observed that, as it was impossible in the nature of things to prevent the examination of the dead body of man, and as there was no law of the Commonwealth regulating the matter, it was manifest the bodies of distinguished legislators themselves, after a life full of good works, were no longer safe in their graves, but were liable to be rudely disturbed.

"After this interview the Senate committee presented an affirmative report.

"When called up on its final passage some days after in the Senate, it was objected that unless the provisions of this Act were restricted to Philadelphia, it ought not to pass, on the ground that the views of the constituents of the rural representatives were not known on the subject.

"The chairman of the college committee being present on the occasion, was asked if it would suit the views of the college to restrict the provisions of the Act of Philadelphia, with the remark that if it did not, the Act probably could not pass. The chairman, being alone at the Capitol at this time, assumed the responsibility of saying that he believed the College of Physicians had the catholic desire of having the benefit of the Act extended to every part of the State, but certainly if it could not be obtained for their neighbors, they would receive it themselves. At the same time he observed it would be well to reflect that from the very title of the Act, 'to prevent the traffic in dead bodies,' if the restriction spoken of was made, while the traffic could not exist in Philadelphia, the converse would be the case in the country, and it would be legal. Yet such was the prejudice against the Act the restriction was made, and when the vote was being taken, a Senator from Allegheny asked to have his district included with Philadelphia, which was done, and the Act passed the Senate.

"It became necessary, on a subsequent visit, to address the same arguments to the members of the House of Representatives, and they approved the action of the Senate.

"The Governor of the State was seen, and made occasion of a third visit to the Capitol, and your committee rejoice to announce our Act became law on the 18th of March 1867.

"It reads as follows:

"'An Act for the Promotion of Medical Science, and to prevent the Traffic in Human Bodies in the City of Philadelphia and the County of Allegheny.

"'Section 1. Be it enacted by the Senate and House of Representatives of the Commonwealth of Pennsylvania, in General Assembly met, and it is hereby enacted by the authority of the same, That any public officer in the City of Philadelphia or the County of Allegheny, having charge thereof or control over the same, shall give permission to any physician or surgeon of the same city or county, upon his request made therefor, to take the bodies of deceased persons required to be buried at public expense, to be by him used within the State for the advancement of medical science, preference being given to medical schools, public and private; and said bodies to be distributed to and among the same, equitably, the number assigned to each being proportioned to that of its students; provided, however, that if the deceased person, during his or her last sickness, of his or her own accord, shall request to be buried; or if any person, claiming to be, and satisfying the proper authorities that he or she is of kindred to the deceased, shall ask to have the body for burial, it shall be surrendered for interment; or if such deceased person was a stranger or traveler, who died suddenly, the body shall be buried, and shall not be handed over as aforesaid.

"'Section 2. Every physician or surgeon, before receiving any such dead body, shall give to the proper authorities surrendering the same to him, a sufficient bond that such body shall be used only for the promotion of medical science within this State, and whosoever shall use such body or bodies for any other purpose, or shall remove the same beyond the limits of this State; and whosoever shall sell or buy such body or bodies, or in any way traffic in the same, shall be deemed guilty of a misdemeanor, and shall, on conviction, be imprisoned for a term not exceeding five years, at hard labor, in the county jail.

(Signed) L.H. Hall,
Speaker of the Senate
John P. Glass
Speaker of House Rep.
Approved March 18th, 1867
John W. Geary, Governor'

"Such is the law obtained from our legislature through the action of this college in its corporate capacity.

"A law, the humane provisions of which were first partially established in Edinburgh in 1505, and yet more extended in France after the revolution of 1798, and under the first empire; and the wisdom of which was observed by the British Parliament in a statute only of late, when a frightful crime revealed its necessity.

"All of which is respectfully submitted.

"Signed by the committee.

Wm. S. Forbes, MD., Chairman

Hall of the College of Physicians

Thirteenth and Locust Streets, April 1867"

On motion of Dr. Rodman, the College of Physicians unanimously passed a vote of thanks for "the able and successful exertions" made to obtain this law.

B: Reports of Societies from the *Cincinnati Lancet and Clinic**

The Academy of Medicine on the Anatomy Act

At a recent meeting of the Academy, its committee, appointed several weeks previous, made the following report:

"Your committee appointed to revise the resolutions referred to them at the meeting two weeks ago, respectfully report the following preamble and resolutions:

"WHEREAS, The existing laws of the State of Ohio are wholly inadequate to the securing of a proper supply of anatomical material for the purpose of teaching and study, and

"WHEREAS, in consequence of such defective legislation, material is and can only be obtained through resurrectionists and the illegal violation of graves, and

"WHEREAS, the medical interests of our State are too important to be jeopardized as they now are under the working of the Anatomy Act of 1870, and

Cincinnati Lancet and Clinic, A Weekly Journal of Medicine and Surgery New Series, Volume 1, 1878, or Whole Series, Vol XL, No. 1, 1878. pp. 8–11.

"WHEREAS, the State demands of medical practitioners a high degree of professional knowledge and skill and at the same time under the present laws refuses the means by which such knowledge can be properly and sufficiently obtained, thereby doing great injustice not only to physicians, but also to all classes of the community since it is the sick upon whom ultimately the evil is wrought, therefore be it

"*Resolved*, By the Academy of Medicine, that a committee of three be appointed by the President to memorialize the Legislature at its next session to pass such law or laws as will enable the legal procuring for the purpose of dissection of any or all bodies of persons dying in public institutions of the State, County infirmaries and City hospitals, such as may at the expiration of a period of twenty-four hours after death remain unclaimed by friends or relatives, and also all bodies found dead which may remain unburied and unclaimed during the period of time above stated, and further be it

"*Resolved*, That it shall be the duty of the same committee of the Academy to secure as far as possible the signatures of the members of the medical profession of Cincinnati and Hamilton County a petition praying the General Assembly of the State of Ohio to pass such law or laws as above indicated, and further be it

"*Resolved*, That a copy of this preamble and resolutions be sent to each and every medical society on the State of Ohio asking cooperation in this matter.

Geo. E. Walton,
J.W. Underhill,
P.S. Connor,

Cincinnati, June 17, 1878."

Annotated Bibliography

Academy of Medicine on the anatomy act. Reports of Societies. *Cincinnati Lancet and Clinic* 1: 8–11, 1878. The full text of this report appears as Appendix B.

Ackerknecht, Erwin H. *A Short History of Medicine*. New York: Ronald Press, 1955. A good, brief introductory text in the history of medicine.

Andrassy, Richard J. and Hagood, Clyde O. Leonardo Da Vinci: anatomist and medical illustrator. *Southern Medical Journal* 69: 787–788, June 1976.

Arey, Leslie B. Resurrection men. *Quarterly Bulletin of Northwestern University Medical School* 14 (4): 209–219, Winter 1940. A review of body snatching activities, primarily English, covering "professionals," methods and techniques, and murder. Scant attention to American activities, but mention is made of both Baltimore and Cincinnati burking cases.

Association of American Anatomists. Extract from Proceedings of Eight Sessions held at Philadelphia, PA, December 27 and 28, 1895. [Reprinted from *Science* (NS), vol. III, January 17, 1896.] The association report consists of three parts: (1) the address of the president, (2) a report from the Committee on Collection and Preservation of Anatomical Material, and (3) the text of the Anatomical Law of the State of Pennsylvania. The Committee agreed that of the anatomical laws in effect in the country in 1895, the Pennsylvania law was the best, providing a model for the promotion of medical science *and* the prevention of desecration of graves.

Atkinson, William B. *The Physicians and Surgeons of the United States.* Philadelphia: Charles Robson, 1878. Over 2600 biographical sketches in this compilation, many accompanied by portraits; an excellent source of material on physicians of the 1800s.

Atwater, Edward C. Making fewer mistakes: a history of students and patients. *Bulletin of the History of Medicine* 57 (2): 165–187, Summer 1983. A critical look at the development of medical education and curriculum. Well referenced.

_____. The protracted labor and brief life of a country medical school; the Auburn Medical Institution. *Journal of the History of Medicine and Allied Sciences* 34 (3): 334-352, July 1979.

Baatz, Simon. A very diffused disposition: dissecting schools in Philadelphia, 1823-1825. *Pennsylvania Magazine of History and Biography* 180: 205-215, 1984. A look at the Independent Anatomy Schools of Philadelphia.

Baldwin, James F. Grave robbing. *Ohio State Medical Journal* 32: 754-757, August 1936. Covers Doctor's Riot 1788, Burke and Hare, Harrison snatch and a few other Ohio cases. No references.

Ball, James Moores. *Sack-'Em-Up Men: An Account of the Rise and Fall of the Modern Resurrectionists*. Edinburgh: Oliver and Boyd, 1928. A well-written, entertaining account of grave robbing activities chiefly confined to England and Scotland with cursory treatment of American grave robbers.

(Baltimore) Sun. December 13,14,18, 1886. Burking in Baltimore.

_____. September 9,10, 1887. Execution of John Thomas Ross.

Barzun, Jacques. *Burke and Hare: The Resurrection Men; A Collection of Contemporary Documents Including Broadsides, Occasional Verses, Illustrations, Polemics, and a Complete Transcript at the Trial*. Metuchen, NJ: Scarecrow Press, 1974. A detailed account of the deeds of William Burke and William Hare, illustrated with facsimile reprints of many documents.

Beall, O.T. and Shryock, Richard H. *Cotton Mather: First Significant Figure in American Medicine*. Baltimore: Johns Hopkins Press, 1954.

Bell, Whitfield J., Jr. Body snatching in Philadelphia. *Journal of the History of Medicine* 23: 108-110, 1968. A reprint of Shippen's denial of grave robbing charges from the Pennsylvania Gazette (1770)

_____. Doctor's riot. New York, 1788. *Bulletin of the New York Academy of Medicine* 47 (12): 1501-1503, December 1971. A reprint of a letter from William Heth to Edmund Randolph describing the riot. A good firsthand report.

Bennett, William. Dr. Warren's possessions. *Harvard Magazine* 89 (6) 24-31, July-August 1987. Dr. Warren's possessions include some interesting preserved anatomical specimens. Many are pictured.

Bettmann, Otto L. *Pictorial History of Medicine*. Springfield: C.C. Thomas, 1956. p. 243. The history contains many illustrations from the "Bettmann archive," a few specific to grave robbing; includes drawings of Burke and Hare; the Doctor's Riot of 1788 in New York.

Billings, John S. Literature and institutions. in Clarke, Edward: *A Century of American Medicine 1776-1876*. New York: Burt Franklin, 1971 (a reprint edition). p. 358. Statistical material on the founding and growth of American medical schools, divided by state, with numbers of graduates to 1876.

Blake, John B. The anatomical lectures of William Shippen, 1776. *Transactions and Studies of the College of Physicians of Philadelphia* 42 (1): 61-66, July 1974.

_____. The development of American Anatomy Acts. *Journal of Medical Education* 30: 431-439, August 1955. A review of the need for and evolution of the anatomy acts in the United States. Discusses representative state legislation. Referenced.

Blanton, Wyndham B. *Medicine in Virginia in the Nineteenth Century*. Richmond: Garrett and Massie, 1933. A very complete, detailed history of Virginia in three volumes. This particular volume comprises only the 1800s and includes a chapter entitled "Anatomy and Grave Robbing" accompanied by footnote references.

Bloch, H. Human dissection: epitome of its evolution. *New York State Journal of Medicine* 77(8): 1340–1342, July 1977. A cursory look at evolution of human dissection from Egypt/Greeks to 1850's.

Bodies for dissection. *British Medical Journal* 2: 379–381, September 6, 1947.

Bodies for dissection in Dublin in 1818. *British Medical Journal* 1: 74, January 16, 1943. John Cheyne's experience reported.

Body snatching in Indiana. *Medical Standard* 25: 644, 1902. Editorial.

Bradford, Charles H. Resurrectionists and spunkers. *New England Journal of Medicine* 294 (24):1331–1332, June 10, 1976. Entertaining, well-written two-page commentary.

Bridie, James. *The Anatomist*. London: Constable and Co., Ltd., 1931. A play; tongue-in-cheek fictionalized account of Burke and Hare.

Brieger, Gert H. A portrait of surgery, Surgery in America, 1875–1889. *Surgical Clinics of North America* 67 (6): 1181–1216, December 1967.

Brookville Jeffersonian. November 12, 1857. Body snatching.

Bryson, Hector. *Doctors, Bodies and Snatchers*. Edinburgh: Cannongate, 1978. A fictional account of the medical education of young physicians in Edinburgh during the era of Robert Knox, Robert Liston and other great anatomists.

Butterfield, William C. A caricaturist of the 18th century anatomists and surgeons. *Surgery, Gynecology and Obstetrics* 144 (4): 587–592, April 1977.

Cadwalader, Thomas. An Essay on the West India Dry Gripes to Which Is Added an Extraordinary Case in Physic. Philadelphia, published by Ben Franklin, 1745. (Also in Major: *Classic Descriptions of Disease*.)

Castiglioni, Arturo. *A History of Medicine*. Translated and edited by E.B. Krum-bhaar, M.D. New York: Alfred A. Knopf, 1941. A good general history of medicine translated from Italian. It includes information on the development of anatomy, both the different schools and the trends in education, accom-panied by representative black and white illustrations.

Centennial Volume of the Transactions of the College of Physicians of Philadelphia. Philadelphia: Dornan, 1887. p. 369. Issued on the 100th anniver-sary of the college and includes a history of the institution, significant events that occurred and personal histories of some of the most famous fellows.

(Cincinnati) Enquirer. February 24, 1884. Confessed. Sickening details of the Avon-dale triple murder.

(Cincinnati) Evening Post. February 22,23, 1884. Avondale mystery solved. Burkers bagged.

Cohen, Ed. Cemetery was fertile ground for med school. *Maryland Today* Fall 1987. (A publication for Alumni, Faculty and Friends of University of Maryland.) The procurement of cadavers for Davidge's classes at Medical School of Maryland by "Frank the Body Snatcher." Shipment of cadavers also mentioned.

Cole, Hubert. *Things for the Surgeon.* London: Heinemann, 1964. A very readable volume that details grave robbing and anatomy primarily in England. Few references.

Cooper, Bransby Blake. *The Life of Sir Astley Cooper, Bart.* London: John W. Parker, 2 volumes. 1843. Two volumes covering the life and escapades of one of the world's greatest surgeons and anatomists. In it, he reveals his activities in grave robbing and his dealings with "professional" resurrectionists.

Cordell, Eugene F. *Medical Annals of Maryland 1799–1889.* Baltimore, 1903.

Corner, Betsy Copping. *William Shippen, Jr., Pioneer in American Medical Education.* Philadelphia: American Philosophical Society, 1951. This is the only book-length biography of William Shippen. It includes Shippen's abbreviated diary/record of daily activities that he kept during his anatomy classes with the Hunters when he studied abroad.

Corner, George W. *Anatomy.* (Clio Medica 3) New York: Hoeber, 1930. A short illustrated history of anatomy from the Greeks to modern times.

Corpse and the beaver hat; one of the *causes célèbres* of Rhode Island, how justice was administered in the beginning of this century. *Rhode Island Medical Journal* 50: 836–846, 855, December 1967. A body snatching that became a political football.

Craven, Thomas (ed.). *A Treasury of Art Masterpieces from the Renaissance to the Present Day.* New York: Simon and Schuster, 1958.

Cummins, Harold. Cadaver procurement by the Tulane School of Medicine, 1834. *Bulletin of the Tulane University Medical Faculty* 26: 13–17, 1967. Grave robbing was not a problem for Tulane. Charity Hospital was nearby and sufficient supplies of unclaimed dead were available.

Dobson, Jessie. The 'Anatomizing' of criminals. *Annals of the Royal College of Surgeons of England* 9: 112–120, 1951. The tradition of public anatomies of criminals is reviewed; drawings of the faces of some of those who suffered this fate are included.

Dulles, C.W. A sketch of the life of Thomas Cadwalader. *Pennsylvania Magazine of History and Biography* 27: 262–278, 1903.

Dunlop, Richard. *Doctors of the American Frontier.* Garden City: Doubleday and Company, 1965.

Edwards, Linden F. *Body Snatching in Ohio during the Nineteenth Century.* Public Library of Fort Wayne and Allen County, 1955. A 25-page pamphlet detailing resurrection activities in Ohio, mostly based on newspaper accounts of the occurrences.

————. Cincinnati's "Old Cunny," a notorious purveyor of human flesh. *Ohio State Medical Journal* 50: 466–469, 1954. The story of William Cunningham, professional resurrectionist.

————. Human dissection. *Ohio State Medical Journal* 40 (4): 331-337, April 1944. A history from the earliest times (Greek/Oriental) culminating with the Harrison case and the Ohio Anatomy Law.

————. The Ohio Anatomy Law of 1881. *Ohio State Medical Journal* 46: 1190–1192, December 1950; 47: 49–52, January 1951; 47: 143–146, February 1951.

_____. Resurrection riots during the heroic age of anatomy in America. *Bulletin of the History of Medicine* 25: 178–184, 1951. A good review of the various resurrection riots with a brief description of each.

Eliot, Llewellin. Comment on Frank Baker's "A History of Bodysnatching." *Washington Medical Annals* 247–253, 1916. A short comment on body snatching in the Washington, D.C., area in which the first evidence of George Christian's diary appears.

Flexner, James Thomas. *Doctors on Horseback: Pioneers of American Medicine.* New York: Garden City Publishing Co., 1939. A collection of seven biographies of American pioneer physicians, their lives, contributions, and exploits.

Forbes, William S. *History of the Anatomy Act of Pennsylvania.* Philadelphia, 1867. Full text appears as Appendix I.

Frank, Julia Bess. Body snatching: a grave medical problem. *Yale Journal of Biology and Medicine* 49 (4): 399–410, September 1976. Traces the legalization of dissection from the 14th century to the enactment of the Warburton Act. Mentions a few American difficulties; the Yale riot of 1824 and the Harrison case.

Gallagher, Thomas. The body snatchers. *American Heritage* 18 (4): 64–73, 1967. A record of the 1788 Doctor's Riot at Columbia College in New York, complete with maps and illustrations.

Geller, Stephen A. Religious attitudes and the autopsy. *Archives of Pathology and Laboratory Medicine* 108 (6): 494–496, June 1984. A review of the attitudes toward autopsy as set forth by each of the world's major religions.

Gerstner, Patsy A. A note on body snatching in the United States. *Bulletin of the Cleveland Medical Library Association* 18: 64–65, July 1971. A reprint of a letter from John D. Godman to John C. Warren comparing cadaver procurement procedures from public grounds in New York and Philadelphia.

Gibson, William. *Rambles in Europe in 1839, with Sketches of Prominent Surgeons, Physicians, Medical Schools, Hospitals, Literary Personages, Scenery, etc.* Philadelphia: Lea and Blanchard, 1841.

Grindle, Jack. Body snatchers. *New Orleans Medical and Surgical Journal* 99: 627–637, June 1947. A review of body snatching from earliest times, with emphasis on the English experience.

Gross, Samuel David. *Autobiography with Sketches of His Contemporaries.* Philadelphia: George Barrie, 1887. Reprint edition: Arno, 1972. A two volume autobiography, one of the most attractive features of which is Gross' descriptions and comments about many of his colleagues. For the purposes of this history, Physick and Mott were of special interest.

Guthrie, Douglas J. *A History of Medicine.* London: Thomas Nelson and Sons, Ltd., 1945. Another good introductory text on history of medicine.

Guttmacher, Alan. *Bootlegging Bodies: A History of Body-Snatching.* Public Library of Fort Wayne and Allen County, 1955. A 57-page booklet that reviews the history of body snatching, the largest portion of which centers on European experiences.

Haggard, Howard W. *Devils, Drugs and Doctors; The Story of the Science of Healing from Medicine-Man to Doctor.* New York: Halcyon House, 1929. Chapter six traces the making of an anatomy from early Egypt to the murders committed by Burke and Hare; includes illustrations and reprints or excerpts of original documents and title pages.

Hamlin, Hannibal. The Dissection Riot of 1824 and the Connecticut Anatomical Law. *Yale Journal of Biology and Medicine* 7 (4) 275–289, 1934–1935. A complete description of the snatch of Bathsheba Smith and the events that followed (the riot) and eventual conviction of the unfortunate Ephraim Colborn.

Hartt, Frederick. *Art: A History of Painting, Sculpture, Architecture; Renaissance, Baroque, Modern World*. New York: Harry N. Abrams, Inc., 1976. Volume 2.

Hartwell, Edward M. The hindrances to anatomical study in the United States, including a special record of the struggles of our early anatomical teachers. *Annals of Anatomy and Surgery* 3: 209–225, 1881. An excellent review of colonial post mortems, first state anatomy laws, William Shippen's anatomy classes, and the Doctor's Riot of 1788. No references.

Haviland, Thomas N. Benjamin Rush, Philip Syng Physick, and the resurrectionists. *Surgery, Gynecology and Obstetrics* 117: 774–776, 1963. The account of a resurrectionist's attempt to sell the body of Benjamin Rush to Philip Syng Physick for use in his class.

_____. How Sir Charles Bell became involved with the "invisible girl." *Transactions and Studies of the College of Physicians of Philadelphia* 42 (3): 268–272, 1975.

Hayward, Oliver S. Three American anatomy letters (1817–1830). *Bulletin of the History of Medicine* 38: 377–378, 1964.

Heaton, Claude: Body snatching in New York City. *New York State Journal of Medicine* 43: 1861–1865, October 1943. Recounts attempts by New York physicians to supply themselves (and their classes) with human bodies for study.

Hektoen, L. Early post-mortem examinations by Europeans in America. *Journal of the American Medical Association* 87: 576–577, 1926. Together with Hoadly, Hosack, Krafka, Krumbhaar (Early history), Krumbhaar (The state), Mather, Matthews, Spiro, and Steiner provide a core of journal information on colonial post mortem examinations.

Henry, Frederick P. Memoir of William S. Forbes, M.D. *Transactions of the College of Physicians of Philadelphia* 29 (series 3): liii–lxiv, 1907.

Hinshaw, William. *A Doctor's Confession*. Des Moines: Baker-Trisler, 1903. Two chapters on cadaver procurement appear early in the book. One mentions Cunningham, the resurrectionist, and his infamous contracts to supply dissecting material to medical colleges.

Hoadly, Charles J. Some early post-mortem examinations in New England. *Proceedings of the Connecticut Medical Society* 207–217, 1892. See Hektoen.

Holloway, Lisabeth M. *Medical Obituaries: American Physicians Biographical Notices in Selected Medical Journals Before 1907*. New York: Garland Publishing, 1981. More than 17,500 physicians' names appear in this biographical compilation, each name followed by one or more references. A prodigious effort.

Holtz, William. Bankrobbers, burkers, and bodysnatchers. *Michigan Quarterly Review* 6 (2): 90–98, 1967. A general review of body snatching relating many of the English stories, but adding some University of Michigan experiences and an account of the James-Younger contribution via the great Northfield bank robbery to the anatomy classes of Michigan.

Hosack, David. Report of Middleton (Peter) and Bard (John) Post-mortem. *American Medical and Philosophical Register* 2: 228, 1812. See Hektoen.

Hubley, Patricia. Disturbing the dead in York, PA. *Susquehanna Monthly Magazine* 15–17, April 1987. During the transfer of bodies from old Potter's Field to a new area, a number of bodies were missing or unaccounted for, P.T. Barnum's circus cannibal among them.

Humphrey, D.C. Dissection and discrimination: the social origins of cadavers in America. 1760–1915. *Bulletin of the New York Academy of Medicine* 49: 819–827, September 1973. A well-referenced paper on the anatomists' proclivity to use the bodies of blacks rather than whites for their studies.

Hunter, R.J. The origin of Philadelphia General Hospital. *Medical Life* (NS) 150: 115–136, 1933.

Jenkins, George B. The legal status of dissecting. *Anatomical Record* 7: 387–399, 1913. A review, based on a survey, of state laws regulating dissection.

Kaufman, Martin and Hanawalt, Leslie L. Body snatching in the Midwest. *Michigan History* 55 (1): 23–40, 1971. Authors make reference to Charles O. Morton (professional body snatcher) being the alias of one Henri Le Caron, M.D., a graduate of Detroit Medical College; personal communication with Dr. Kaufman confirmed that all the evidence to support this conclusion was included in the article.

Keim, deB. Randolph. *Washington, What To See, and How To See It. A Sightseer's Guide.* Washington, D.C., 1892. Street maps and pictures give a sense of "location" for George Christian's business ventures as described in his diary.

Kelly, Howard A. The barred road to anatomy. *Bulletin of the Johns Hopkins Hospital* 19: 196–201, 1908. A mixture of British and American activities in body snatching and murder. Letters and poetry excerpted. No references.

————. and Burrage, Walter L.: *Dictionary of American Medical Biography.* New York: Appleton, 1928. Reprint edition: Longwood, 1979. The "Bible" of historical medical biographies.

Krafka, Joseph. Some early autopsies in Georgia. *American Journal of Surgery* 42: 445–447, November 1938. See Hektoen.

Krumbhaar, Edward B. Early history of anatomy in the United States. *Annals of Medical History* IV: 271–286, 1922. See Hektoen.

————. History of the autopsy and its relation to the development of modern medicine. *Hospitals* 12: 68–74, 1938. A worldwide review of the contributions of autopsy to the study of disease.

————. The history of pathology at the Philadelphia General Hospital. *Medical Life* (NS) 151:162–177, 1933.

————. *Pathology.* (Clio Medica 19) reprint of 1937 edition. AMS Press.

————. The state of pathology in the British colonies of North America. *Yale Journal of Biology and Medicine* 19: 801–815, 1947. See Hektoen.

Ladenheim, J.C. The Doctor's mob of 1788. *Journal of the History of Medicine* V: 23–43, 1950. An hour by hour record of the riot and its aftermath.

Lassek, A.M. *Human Dissection; Its Drama and Struggle*. Springfield: C.C. Thomas, 1958. Probably the most complete book on the development of human anatomical study that exists; excellent bibliography and index.

Late horrible murders in Edinburgh, to obtain subjects for dissection. *Lancet* I: 424,431, 1828–1829. A report on the Burke and Hare murders.

Lawrence, Charles. *History of the Philadelphia Almshouses and Hospitals*. A reprint of 1905 edition. New York: Arno, 1976. A chronological study of the founding and development of the Philadelphia Almshouse, cemetery, burial vault, etc.

Lawrence, Christopher. Alexander Monro Primus and the Edinburgh manner of anatomy. *Bulletin of the History of Medicine* 62 (2) 193–214, Summer 1988.

Laws of Ohio 1870. p. 25–26. An Act to Encourage the Study of Anatomy.

Laws of Ohio 1881. p. 33. Revised Statutes of Ohio Anatomy Law.

Laws of Pennsylvania 1849. p. 397. Act No. 296. To prevent the opening of streets or public roads through burial grounds, and for the protection of cemeteries and graveyards.

Laws of Pennsylvania 1855. p. 462–463. Act No. 494. To protect burial grounds.

Laws of Pennsylvania 1867. p. 497. Act No. 482. (Armstrong Act.) For the promotion of medical science, and to prevent traffic in human bodies, in the City of Philadelphia and County of Allegheny.

Laws of Pennsylvania 1883. p. 119–121. Act No. 106. (Pennsylvania Anatomy Act.) For the promotion of medical science by the distribution and use of unclaimed human bodies for scientific purposes through a board created for that purpose and to prevent unauthorized uses and traffic in human bodies.

Leighton, Alexander. *The Court of Cacus: or, The Story of Burke and Hare*. 2d ed. London: Houlston and Wright, 1861. A fictional account of Burke and Hare, but probably the best account of all those produced.

Life of Sir Robert Christison, Bart. edited by his sons. Edinburgh: William Blackwood & Sons, 2 volumes, ca. 1880. A two volume biography of Christison, with detailed accounts of his grave robbing adventures. He seemed sufficiently knowledgable of the techniques to have personally participated.

Long, Esmond R. *A History of American Pathology*. Springfield: C.C. Thomas, 1962. The early chapters deal with the development of anatomy/dissection.

Lonsdale, Henry. *A Sketch of the Life and Writings of Robert Knox, The Anatomist*. London: Macmillan and Co., 1870.

Lytton, Edward Bulwer (Lord). *Lucretia; or The Children of Night*. London, etc. Fiction.

McAlister, Neil H. John Hunter and the Irish giant. *Canadian Medical Association Journal* 111: 256–257, August 3, 1974. Grave watchers bribed to give up the body of the Irish giant.

McDaniel, W.B., 2d. John Jones' introductory lecture to his course in surgery (1769), King's College, Printed from the author's manuscript. *Transactions of the College of Physicians of Philadelphia* 4th series. 8: 180–190, 1940–1941.

Macilwain, George. *Memoirs of John Abernethy, F.R.S., with a view of his lectures, writings, and character*. 2d. ed., London: Hurst and Blackett, 1854.

McMurrich, J. Playfair: *Leonardo Da Vinci, The Anatomist*. Baltimore: Williams and Wilkins, 1930.

Major, Ralph H. *Classic Descriptions of Disease*. 3d ed. Springfield: C.C. Thomas, 1978. Bard's description of diphtheria with report of three post mortems.

Mann, Ruth J. Regnier de Graff, 1641–1673, Investigator. *Fertility and Sterility*. 27 (4): 466–468, April 1976.

Mather, Cotton. *Magnalia Christi Americana; of the Ecclesiastical History of New England; from its first planting, in the year 1620, unto the year of our Lord 1698*. In seven books. New York: Russell and Russell, 1967. See Hektoen.

Matthews, Albert. Notes on early autopsies and anatomical lectures. Colonial Society of Massachusetts. *Publications* 19: 273–290, 1918. See Hektoen.

Middleton, William S. William Osler and the Blockley Dead House. *Journal-Oklahoma State Medical Association* 69 (6): 387–397, September 1976.

————. William Shippen, Junior. *Annals of Medical History* (NS) (Part 1) 4: 440–456, September 1932.

————. William Shippen, Junior. *Annals of Medical History* (NS) (Part 2, Conclusion) 4: 538–549, November 1932. With above, a biography of the life of William Shippen, Jr.

Mitchell, G.A.G. Anatomical and resurrectionist activities in northern Scotland. *Journal of the History of Medicine and Allied Science* 4: 417–430, 1949 Anatomical events centering on Aberdeen University. Most interesting aspect of this paper is its attention to modes of prevention of body snatching.

Moir, David Macbeth. *The Life of Mansie Wauch: Tailor in Dalkeith*. London: T.N. Foulis, 1911. A fictional account, the only one that deals with the employment of grave watchers to deter the body snatchers on their nightly rounds.

Montgomery, H. A body-snatcher sponsors Pennsylvania's Anatomy Act. *Journal of the History of Medicine* 21: 374–393, 1966. The story of an inept grave robbery and a physician-participant's role in the revision of the Pennsylvania Anatomy Act of 1867.

Norris, George W. *Early History of Medicine in Philadelphia*. Philadelphia: W. F. Norris, 1886. A collection of biographies and accounts of medical events in Philadelphia 1700–1800; includes report of Shippen's early anatomy classes and his admission that he sometimes obtained his specimens from Potter's Field.

Norwood, William Frederick. *Medical Education in the United States before the Civil War*. Philadelphia: University of Pennsylvania Press, 1944. Very probably the "classic" on development of American medical education. Also details the resurrection riots.

Packard, Francis R. *History of Medicine in the United States*. 2 volumes. New York: Hafner, 1963. p. 298–301; p. 786–787.One of the very best histories of American medicine with footnotes and bibliography. A real work of writing art and historical research.

————. The practice of medicine in Philadelphia in the eighteenth century. *Annals of Medical History* 5 (n.s.) (2): 135–150, March 1933. Treats the development of medical colleges and hospitals, well-known practitioners of Philadelphia. Some attention given to medical education and apprenticeship; comments on Shippen and his anatomy classes.

_____. The resurrectionists of London and Edinburgh. *Medical News* 81: 64, 1902. Covers resurrectionists, murders, bribery of grave watchers, poetry and some fictional works on body snatching.

Pennsylvania Gazette. November 11, 1762; September 26, 1765; January 11, 1770. Shippen's letters.

(Philadelphia) Public Ledger. June 8, 1839. Adventures in a graveyard.

_____. May 17, 1841. Human head.

_____. September 6, 1841. Medical Department of the Pennsylvania College.

_____. September 26, 1841. Sanctity of the grave desecrated.

_____. October 13, 1846. Excitement — dead body found.

_____. December 6,7,8,14,15,16,18, 1882. The Jefferson story.

Robert Knox and the body snatchers. *Medical Journal of Australia* 2: 929–930, November 27, 1965. A sympathetic view of Robert Knox as the victim of a scandal for which he had no real responsibility.

Robinson, John Hovey. *Marietta, or the Two Students, a Tale of the Dissecting Room and Body Snatching*. Boston: Jordan and Wiley, 1846. (On microfilm from Research Publications but probably an incomplete version.) Fiction.

Robinson, Victor. *The Story of Medicine*. New York, Tudor, 1931.

Rothstein, William G. *American Medical Schools and the Practice of Medicine: A History*. New York: Oxford, 1987. A modern Norwood (above) and likely to be a classic on American medical education; well referenced.

Roughhead, William. "The Wolves of the Westport" (1938) in *The Murder's Companion*. New York: Reader's Club. Fiction.

Samuel Clossy, M.D.; Existing Works with a Biographical Sketch. Saffron, Morris H. New York: Hafner, 1967. One of the few works on Samuel Clossy, the biographical sketch is well-written, complete, and referenced. Clossy's book, *Observations on Some of the Diseases of the Parts of the Human Body. Chiefly taken from the Dissections of Morbid Bodies* (1763) is reprinted in its entirety and constitutes the second half of this work.

Savitt, Todd L. The use of blacks for medical experimentation and demonstration in the Old South. *Journal of Southern History* 48 (3): 331–348, August 1982. A well-researched history of the use of blacks in the South not only for anatomical dissection but for experimental surgical procedures.

Sievers, Harry J. *Benjamin Harrison: Hoosier Statesman. from the Civil War to the White House. 1865–1888*. Volume 2. New York: University Publications, Inc. Chapter 10, "The Harrison Horror." The body snatching of John Scott Harrison, father of Benjamin Harrison.

Singer, Charles. Notes on Renaissance artists and practical anatomy. *Journal of the History of Medicine and Allied Science* 5: 156–162, 1950.

_____. *The Evolution of Anatomy: A Short History of Anatomy and Physiology from the Greeks to Harvey*. New York: Alfred A. Knopf, 1925. An illustrated history of anatomy with emphasis on the early European schools and teachers.

Smith, Aquilla. On teaching anatomy in America. *Dublin Journal of Medical Science* 17: 218–221, 1840. Contains a reprint of Samuel Clossy's letter to George Cleghorn (1764).

Smith, Raymond A., Jr. Of cadavers, chases and colleges. Newspaper coverage, 1885. *Minnesota History* 49 (8): 332–337, Winter 1985. An account of a body snatching ending in a winter night chase through the Minnesota woods.

Smout, C.F.V. The story of the resurrectionists. *Cambridge University Medical Society Magazine* 23: 76–83, 1946. A potpourri of English body snatching stories. Mentions trade in teeth.

Some account of the schools of medicine, hospitals, dispensaries, private lectures, and other means of imparting medical instruction in the city of Philadelphia. *Medical and Surgical Reporter* 3: 9–23, October 1, 1859. A list of medical colleges, practical anatomy classes, hospitals and special lectures, including locations, fees and lecturers.

Southey, Robert. *Joan of Arc, Ballads, Lyrics, and Minor Poems.* London: George Routledge and Sons. p. 275–280. A collection of poems including "The Surgeon's Warning."

Sozinsky, Thomas S. Grave-robbing and dissection. *Penn Monthly* 10:206–217, March 1879. A general history with emphasis on American anatomy legislation in several states.

Spiro, Robert K. A backward glance at the study of postmortem anatomy. Part 2. *International Surgery* 56 (2):101–112, August 1971. See Hektoen.

Steiner, W.R. Some early autopsies in the United States. *Johns Hopkins Hospital Bulletin* 14: 201–203, August 1903. See Hektoen.

Stevenson, Robert Louis. "The Body Snatcher." 1884. A fictional short story based on the Burke and Hare scandal and Robert Knox's role.

Stookey, Byron. Samuel Clossy, A.B., M.D., F.R.C.P. of Ireland; First Professor of Anatomy, King's College (Columbia), New York. *Bulletin of the History of Medicine* 38: 153–167, March-April 1964.

Stringham, James S. Post-mortem instructions outlined in *American Medical and Philosophical Register* 4: 614–615, 1814.

Tait, H.P. Some Edinburgh medical men at the time of the resurrectionists. *Edinburgh Medical Journal* 55: 116–123, February 1948. Discussion of Knox, Cooper, Monro, Bell, Barclay, Liston, etc., and how they dealt with the resurrectionists.

Taylor, Douglass W. The manuscript-lecture notes of Alexander Monro Primus (1697–1767). *Medical History* 30 (4): 444–467, October 1986.

Thomas, Dylan. *The Doctor and the Devils.* New York: Time, Inc., 1964. A play based on Burke and Hare theme, but of a much more serious nature than Bridie's *The Anatomist.*

Thomas Wakley, the founder of the *Lancet.* A biography. *Lancet* I: 185–187, January 18, 1896.

Thompsett, D.H. Anatomical injections. *Annals of the Royal College of Surgeons of England* 45: 108–115, 1969. A study of the early (1600–1830) methods of cadaver preservation by injection and the use of injection today.

Van Ingen, Philip. *The New York Academy of Medicine: Its First Hundred Years.* New York, 1949.

Waite, Frederick C. Early development of anatomical laws in New England. *New England Journal of Medicine* 233: 716–726, 1945.

_____. An episode in Massachusetts in 1818 related to the teaching of anatomy. *New England Journal of Medicine* 220 (6): 221-227, February 9, 1939. A general review of body snatching in New England and laws, leading into the snatch of Sally Andrews and the conviction of Dr. Thomas Sewall.

_____. Grave robbing in New England. *Bulletin of the Medical Library Association* 33: 272-294, 1945. The most useful, well-organized and thoroughly referenced journal article on American grave robbing.

_____. The second medical school in Ohio, at Worthington 1830-1840. *Ohio State Medical Journal* 33: 1334-1336, 1937.

Walsh, James J. *History of Medicine in New York, Three Centuries of Medical Progress.* New York: National Americana Society, 1919.

Warren, Edward. *The Life of John Collins Warren, M.D. compiled chiefly from his Autobiography and Journals.* Boston: Ticknor and Fields, 1860. Contains several detailed descriptions of grave robbing. Some seem farfetched, but physicians were amateurs so the accounts are quite likely to be accurate.

Warren, Samuel. *Passages from the Diary of a Late Physician.* New York: Harper and Brothers, 1845. (Volume 2).

Washington Directory. 1873.

(Washington) Evening Star. December 15, 16, 18, 1873. The resurrection business.

Washington Post. February 20, 1986. Cemeteries give history lessons.

Wistar, Caspar. Eulogium on William Shippen, M.D., delivered before the College of Physicians of Philadelphia, March 1809. *Philadelphia Journal of Medical and Physical Sciences* 5: 173-188, 1822.

Woodburne, Russell T. Anatomical materials and anatomical laws. *Bulletin for Medical Research of the National Society for Medical Research* 8 (5): 2-5, 1954. A collection of anatomy laws from the states with medical schools. With Jenkins and Association of American Anatomists, makes a very good review of anatomy legislation.

Wright-St. Clair, R.E. Murder for anatomy. *New Zealand Medical Journal* 60: 64-69, February 1961. Deals with three English murder scandals giving more attention to Torrence and Waldie and Bishop, May, and Williams and less to Burke and Hare.

(York) Dispatch. April 5 through 9, 1897. Relocation of Potter's Field and disappearance of the body of the cannibal.

Index

A.H. Jones and Company
60
*Academicarum Annota-
tionium* (Albinus) 4
Agnew, David Hayes 6, 18
Agnew Clinic 6
Albinus, Bernhard S. 4
American Medical Assoc.
6
Anatomic teaching mate-
rial, shortage of 14, 15
Anatomical injection 19
Anatomist (Bridie) 108
Anatomy: malpractice 19;
teaching of 18
Anatomy Act: Connec-
ticut, 1833 78; Massa-
chusetts, 1784 78; Mich-
igan, 1844 78; New
Hampshire, 1834 78;
New York 78; New
York, 1789 80; Pennsyl-
vania, 1867 82
*Anatomy of the Gravid
Uterus* (Hunter) 21
Anatomy schools 18
Andrews, Sally 51
Armstrong, General 80
Armstrong Act (1867) 85
Association of American
Anatomists 91, 92

Baltimore Resurrection
Riot 46
Banks, Gen. Nathaniel P.
54
Bard, John 13
Bard, Samuel 5
Battle of the Ten Nudes
(Pollaiuolo) 1
Bayley, Richard 39, 78
Bell, Sir Charles 99
Benham, Dr. 81
Beverly, Thomas 60
Bishop, John 70
Blacks, anatomic study 39
Blockson, Mary 72–73
Blockson, Sarah 73
Board of Buzzards, Phila-
delphia Almshouse 28
Boardman 64, 67
Boarman, Charles V. 67
"Body Snatcher" (Steven-
son) 105
Bodye, Edward, deceased,
autopsy of 10
*Boekelman, President of
the Society* (Pool) 3
Boerhaave, Hermann 4
Bribery for bodies 27
Bridge, John, autopsy of
10
Bridgeman, Edward L. 45

Brown, Emily 72
Brown, Marshall J.A. 74
Brown, Owen 54
Brown, Percy 61
Brown (or Pratt), Maude
61
Burke (Burking), defini-
tion of x
Burke, William 69
Butler, factotum 57
Butler, Tom 57–58
Byrne (or O'Brien),
Charles, resurrection
of 42

Cadaver procurement
operations 37
Cadaver producing
contracts 37
Cadaver shipment 37, 38
Cadwalader, Thomas 12
Call, autopsy of 10
Carmichael, George 82
Carpue, Joseph C. 99
Carroll, Hermanus 13
Casseri, Guilio 3
Cassiday, Patrick 46
Cemeteries: most suscepti-
ble to body snatchers
35; paupers 35; potter's
fields 35; private 36;

private, St. Mary's Church 36
Chew, Levi 81
Chew, Robert 81
Cheyne, John 32
Christian, George (Dr. S.E. French) 37, 38, 61
Christison, Sir Robert 33
Cleghorn, George 11
Clossy, Samuel 10–11
Clow, Roderick F. 97
Colborn, Ephraim 47
Columbo, Realdo 2
Congressional Cemetery 63, 66
Cooper, Sir Astley 33,43, 56, 87, 99
Cooper, Bransby Blake 57
Court of Cacus, The Story of Burke and Hare... (Leighton) 107
Cox, Joseph 13
Cunningham, William 59
Curriculum development, medical 17; anatomy as a force in 17

Dallas, John 72
Dandy, John 9
Darwin, Charles 45
Davidge, John Beale 46
Davis, Dr. 66
Davis, J.S., University of Virginia 37–38
Davis, John Staige 68
Death of Christ (Mantegna) 3
deGraaf, Regnier 4
De Humani Corporis Fabrica (Vesalius) 3
De Mulierum Organis Generationi Inservientibus 4
Desecration at St. Mary's Church 36
Deterrents to resurrection: churchyard walls 44; grave marking 44; iron coffins 45; mortsafes 45; planks 44; quicklime 44; stones 44; trip lines 45
Deuteronomy, Biblical prohibition of autopsy 7
Devin, Augustus 60, 85
De Virorum Organis Generationi Inservientibus 4

Diary of a Late Physician (Warren) 42
Diary of a Resurrectionist (Bailey) 62
Disinterment: effect of weather conditions 35; time of night 35; time of year 35
Disinterment, methods of 31; hooking 32; levering off the lid 33
Docherty, Madgy 70
Doctor and the Devils (Thomas) 108
Doctor's Riot (1788) 79
Doctors of the American Frontier (Dunlop) 53
Doctors, Bodies, and Snatchers (Bryson) 95
Dorrance, John 48–49
Dueling 8

Eakins, Thomas 6
Eaton, George 85
Eaton, L.S. 60
Ebenezar Church and Cemetery 64, 67
An Essay on the West-India Dry Gripes (Cadwalader) 12

Fabrica (Vesalius) 2
Fallopius, Gabriel 3
Fenner, Arthur 48
Ferrari, Carlo 71
Ferryman, Philadelphia Almshouse 28
Finley, Samuel 21
Fisherman, definition of ix
Fletcher, Thomas, resurrected 61
Forbes, William Smith 18, 81, 82, 83; private school of anatomy 82
Fothergill, John 21
Fraser, George 13
Frothingham, Dr. 65
Frothingham, G.E. 38, 67

Gailey, C.P. 55
Ghastly Act 85
Glenwood Cemetery 64, 67
Godman, John D. 18
Goodale, Jacob, autopsy of 10
Grabs, definition of ix

Grave robbers, definition of ix
Grave watchers 41, 42
Gray, Mr. and Mrs. 70
Green, Charles 62
Green, medical student 55
Grimes, John 13
Gross, Samuel David 6, 19, 55
Guy's Hospital 99

Hamilton, Alexander 79
Hare, William 69
Harlan, Herbert 73
Harmony Cemetery 64, 67
Harnett, resurrectionist 57
Harper's Ferry 54
Harris, Grandison 39
Harrison, Benjamin 85
Harrison, John Scott, resurrected 85
Harrison, John, son of John Scott Harrison 85
Harrison, Margaret 61
Harrison, William Henry 85
Hawkins, Albert 73
Hazen, David Henry 67
Henderson, William 81
Hercules and Antaeus (Pollaiuolo) 1
Heth, Colonel William 79
Heyl, Irwin 60
Hickman, Beau 62
Hill, William 71
Hilliard, Cap 60
History of the Anatomy Act of Pennsylvania 83, 111–117
Holmead's Cemetery 61, 63, 66
Holmes, Oliver Wendell, on dissection 18
Humanio 79
Hunter, John 2, 21, 42
Hunter, William 5, 21
Hydrocephalic child, resurrection of 41

Imposters, used in acquiring bodies 26, 27
Ingalls, Allen 75
Ingalls, Richard 75
Ingalls, William 30
Injection, anatomical 18–19
Invisible Girl (Hood) 98
Iron coffins 45

J.D. Quimby and Company 65
James-Younger gang 54
Janssen 60
Jay, John, wounded in Doctor's Riot (1788) 80
Jefferson Medical College and body snatching 81
Jenty, anatomical models 21
John Brown's raid 54
Johnson, Benjamin 75
Johnston, Andrew 12
Jones, John 19
Julian, an Indian, anatomy of 13

Keen, William W. 6
Kelley, Elizabeth, died by witchcraft, autopsy of 9
Kerfbyle, Johannes 10
Knight, Jonathan 47
Knox, Robert 70; introductory lecture of 96; reputation and personality 106

Lack of bodies, obstacle to anatomic teaching 15
Lambert, Emma Jane 74
Lawrence, Jason Valentine O'Brien 18
Lebanon Cemetery 81
Le Caron, Henry 60
Lee, Alice, wife of Shippen 24
Lees (or Merrilees), Andrew 26
Leonardo da Vinci 2
Lesson in Anatomy of Dr. John Deyman (Rembrandt) 3
Lesson in Anatomy of Dr. Tulp (Rembrandt) 3
Life of Mansie Wauch, Tailor in Dalkeith (Moir) 110
Linnard, member of the Board of Philadelphia Almshouse 29
Loftas, John 101
Logue (Laird, Log), Maggie 69
Lohman, Dr. 81
Lout, Jeff, arrested 75
Lucretia; or the Children of Night (Lytton) 104

McDougal, Helen 69
McDowell, Joseph N. 50
McDowell Medical College Resurrection Riot 48
Mack, Johnny 61
Mackenzie, Colin 21
McKnight, Charles 78
McNamee, Frank 81
Magnalia Christi Americana Book III (Mather) 10
Mala praxis 19
Malpractice 19
Mantegna, Andrea 3
Marietta (Robinson) 96
Marshall, A.Q., janitor 86
Marshall, Chief Justice John 51
Mary's Ghost: A Pathetic Ballad (Hood) 98–99
Massachusetts Law (1784) 8
Mather, Cotton 10
Mather, Katherine, autopsy of 10
May, John, burker 70
Megargee, Louis N., city editor, *Philadelphia Press* 81
Memoirs of John Abernethy, and malpractice 19
Methodist Cemetery 64, 67
Michelangelo 1
Middleton, Peter 13
Miller, William, autopsy of 12
Moldewarp (or Mole) 27
Monro, Alexander, Primus 4
Monro, Alexander, Tertius 70
Monro, John 4
Monro anatomical dissection 4–5
Monro course outline 4
Morgan, John 5, 14, 24
Morton, Charles O. 60, 86
Morton, Henry 60
Mosely, E.B., member of Board of Philadelphia Almshouse 28
Mott, Valentine 49
Mt. Zion Cemetery 66, 68
Mullen, Andrew "Yank," 81

Naples, Joseph 62
New York Anatomy Riot 46
Northfield, Minnesota, bank robbery 54

Observationes Anatomicae (Fallopius) 3
Observations on Some of the Diseases. . . (Clossy) 10–11
Ohio Anatomy Law, 1870 87; amended 1881 88–89
Osborn, Erastus 47
Otis, George A. 62

P.T. Barnum's cannibal, disinterred 36
Paaw, Pieter 3
Pancoast, Joseph 82
Pancoast, William 6
Partridge, Mr., King's College demonstrator in anatomy 71
Paterson, Mary 70
Peerce, John 9
Pennsylvania Act No. 296, 1849, illegal disinterment 84
Pennsylvania Act No. 482, 1867, anatomy law 84–85
Pennsylvania Act No. 494, 1855, protection of burial grounds 84
Pennsylvania Anatomy Act No. 106, 1883 85
Percy, Marmaduke 9
Performing an anatomy 18
Perry, Anderson 73
Philadelphia Almshouse 27
Philadelphia Anatomical Riot 22, 46
Philadelphia Anatomical Rooms 18
Philadelphia Association for Medical Instruction 18
Physick, Philip Syng 50
Pigburn, Frances 71
Pillet, Henry "Dutch," 81
Pollaiuolo, Antonio 1
Pool, Juriaen 3
Pope Alexander V 7
Portrait of Professor Gross (Gross Clinic) (Eakins) 6
Post, Wright 78

Post mortems, legally recognized 9
Prevention of body snatching 41
Price, Benjamin, autopsy of 9
Public anatomies 13
Pugh, William H., County Prosecutor, Cincinnati 76

Quimby and Son 68

Rambles in Europe (Gibson) 97
Ramsay, Alexander 13
Randloph, Edmund 79
Religious objections to autopsy 7
Rembrandt 3
Resolution concerning the Ohio Anatomy Act 117–118
Resurrection, definition of x
Resurrection Riot, New York, 1788 78–80
Resurrection riots 45
Rock Creek Church Cemetery 64, 67
Ross, John Thomas 73, 74
Rossiter, Bryan 9
Runge, Emil 73
Rush, Benjamin 51; remarks about Shippen 25
Ruth Sprague, epitaph 97

Sack-em-up-men, definition of ix
St. Mary Axe, home of Sir Astley Cooper 57
St. Mary-le-Bone, burial ground 99
St. Mary's Church Cemetery 36
Salueva, Thomas 55
Schleimer (or Schlimer), Dr. 62, 66
Sewall, Thomas 51
Shaw, Charlie 61
Shillock, Paul 55
Shippen, Nancy, daughter of William Shippen, Jr. 25

Shippen, Thomas Lee, son of William Shippen, Jr. 25
Shippen, William, Jr. 5, 14, 25; denial of body snatching 23; disclaimer of grave robbing 22; first professor of anatomy 21, 24; lectures in anatomy (1762) 22
Signorelli, Luca 1
Simons, J.G. 40
Slaughter, Governor of New York, autopsy of 10
Smith, Bathsheba 47
Smith, Chief Medical Officer, Philadelphia Almshouse 28
Smith, Sydney 5
Snatches, definition of ix
Soldier's Home 64, 67
Sozinsky, Thomas S., malpractice and criminality 20
Spigelius, Adrian 3
Spoon, body snatcher 27
Stansley, John 9
Steuben, Baron, wounded in Doctor's Riot (1788) 80
Stog, Andreas 3
Stone, Samuel, autopsy of 10
Surgeon's Warning (Southey) 99–104
Survey of medical schools and anatomy laws (1913) 92
Survey of medical schools and anatomy laws (1954) 93–94
Sutherland, Henry 40

Tabulae Anatomicae (Casseri) 3
Tale of Two Cities (Dickens) 109
Taylor, Beverly 74
Taylor, Elizabeth 74
Teeth 57
Torrence, Helen 72

van Leeuwenhoek, Anton 4

van Rymsdyck, crayon anatomical drawings 21
Verheyden, Philip 4
Vesalius, Andreas 2

Wakley, Thomas 20; on disinterment 33–34
Waldie, Jean 72
Warren, John 29; on unclaimed bodies 29
Warren, John Collins: and body snatching 29–30; and embalming 19; students of, and body snatching 30, 31
Warren, Samuel 42
Washington Asylum Cemetery 62, 66
Waterhouse, Benjamin 5
Webster, A.H.C., resurrected 62
Webster, Daniel 52
Weideman, Dr. 53
Weisenthal, Charles F. 46
Wepfer, Johann Jacob 4
Wheeler, Henry 54
Whetlie, Elizabeth, autopsy of 10
White, Joshua E., published autopsy record 13
Williams, Thomas 70
Willoughby Medical College Resurrection Riot 48
Wilson, James (Daft Jamie) 70
Wistar, Caspar 24
Wolves of the Westport (Roughhead) 106
Woods, Hiram 73
Workhouse Kate 61
Worthington Medical College Resurrection Riot 48
Wright, Thomas 62
Wright, Thomas, presidential address 91

Yale Medical College Riot 47
Young Men's Cemetery 65, 68

Zanesville, Ohio, Resurrection Riot 47